# THE TRAINS WE LOVED

Prometheus Unbound: The eight-foot single *Prometheus*, here seen leaving Twerton Tunnel, was built in 1888, the last of a famous line of broad-gauge engines on the Great Western Railway

# The TRAINS
# WE LOVED

by C. HAMILTON ELLIS

London
GEORGE ALLEN & UNWIN LTD

First Published in 1947

Printed in Great Britain
in 12 point Baskerville type
by Unwin Brothers Limited
London    and    Woking

WHEN the police want a man, they circulate particulars of his principal features and leading dimensions. If these were all one had to go upon, the man might well remain untroubled. But when George Borrow said of someone that he had a regular petty-larceny look about him, you could have picked out that man from a whole bus load. Tennyson gave us a detailed description of Maud, but it was not the police sort of description. We are left guessing her exact height and weight. But we learn that she had an exquisite face and a beautiful voice, then that she was tall and stately, and finally that she was Queen Rose in the rosebud garden of girls. There was Maud, alive and exciting.

This book is not about people but about things. Yet of all things that man has made, the steam train—and perhaps the aeroplane—are most apparently alive. Moreover, while to an onlooker the aeroplane seems perpetually angry, a cross, buzzing, busy thing, the train is decent, even benevolent. She rushes smiling through the summer meadows, laughs in austere mountain places, defies the lugubrious tunnel with a shriek of delight. Of course, the friendliest trains were those we knew as boys; to-day, the branch train to Lyme Regis, or Framlingham, or Ballachulish, receives the returning wanderer like an old nurse. This is not a reference book, but a sympathetic attempt to recall what the old British railway systems, and their trains, were really like.

In making this essay, and in compiling its illustrations, I have been helped by many colleagues and friends, of whom I would mention, in particular, Messrs. A. R. Bell (*The Locomotive*), W. C. Brudenell (L.M.S.R.), Dr. T. F. Budden, Messrs. C. R. Clinker (Locomotive and General Railway Photographs), George Dow (L.N.E.R.), C. Grasemann (Southern Railway), O. J. Morris, Anthony Murray, K. A. C. R. Nunn, and W. H. Whitworth.

C. H. E.

# CONTENTS

# ILLUSTRATIONS IN COLOUR

## Illustrations

Down Continental Express near Bickley, London Chatham and Dover Railway, hauled by William Kirtley's bogie engine No. 12.

Dugald Drummond's No. 292, L.S.W.R., and Stroudley's *Cleveland*, L.B.S.C.R., at Portsmouth.

Train from Ryde, headed by Beyer Peacock 2–4–0 tank engine No. 5, I.W.C.R.

Up West of England Express, Drummond T 9 4–4–0 No. 122 with invalid saloon, L.S.W.R.

Down Bournemouth Express, Drummond "Paddlebox" four-cylinder 4–6–0 No. 447, L.S.W.R.

Victoria–Eastbourne express, hauled by Marsh Atlantic No. 40 (first series, unsuperheated).

*between pages* 96–97

Survivor of the Salisbury Smash: Drummond 4–4–0 No. 421, L.S.W.R.

G.W.R. boat express hauled by a "City" and a "Bulldog."

Broad-gauge Days: a local train with one of the 10 ft. 6 in. wide coaches of 1877 at the rear, G.W.R.

Great Western eight-foot single on mixed-gauge track.

Badminton on up South Wales express, G.W.R.

Southbound train hauled by 4–4–4 tank No. 18, M.S.W.J.R.

S. W. Johnson's small wheeled 4–4–0 type, S.D.J.R.

Paddington–Bristol Express hauled by G. J. Churchward's unique Pacific engine, No. 111, *The Great Bear*.

A characteristic Great Central express of the nineteen-hundreds, hauled by Robinson 4–4–0 locomotive No. 1040.

Goods train at Manchester: Engine No. 471 piloted by saddle tank No. 275 B, G.C.R.

Train from Towcester at Stratford, E. and W.J.R.

Haverhill–Chappel train, 2–4–2 tank No. 3, C.V. and H.R.

North Eastern royal train hauled by Wilson Worsdell's 4–6–0 No. 2010.

London and North Western royal train, headed by Lancashire, Derbyshire and East Coast 0–6–2 tank engine No. 26.

Matthew Stirling's express engine No. 10, H. and B.R.

Down West of England express, Adams' seven-footer No. 594, L.S.W.R.

One of Aspinall's Highflyers in action, L. and Y.R.

# Illustrations

# CHAPTER ONE

# JOURNEYS

SURELY it was always summer when we made our first
railway journeys! Only from later boyhood do we remember
what fog was like at Liverpool Street, with the little North
London engines puffing high-up and unseen, in and out of
Broad Street next-door, and with the Westinghouse pumps of the
Great Eastern panting so furiously amid the Plutonian murk
close at hand; or what a rainy autumnal evening could be like
at Cowlairs; or how the Thames Valley looked between Didcot
and Oxford when there was naught but steel-grey water upon
the drowned meadows. No, it was always summer! Sun shone
on the first blue engine to be seen, a Somerset and Dorset near
Poole; there was sunshine, most dazzling, on a Great Western
brass dome; the sun shone on an extraordinary mustard-
coloured engine of the London, Brighton and South Coast, seen,
according to later detective research, by three-year-old eyes at
Three Bridges, and he certainly shone upon the London and
South Western!

Is this a nostalgic beginning? If so, why not? Everyone who
has loved a train has had his favourite railway, the first one he
ever saw, and mine was that magical South Western. Afterwards
we had our false favourites: the London and North Western
because loving schoolfellows told us, with menaces, that it was
the Premier Line, whatever that might mean; the Midland
because it had red locomotives, and carriages which gave
superlatively comfortable travel; the Great Western because it
had achieved, on excellent authority, 102 miles an hour in 1904.
But most of us went back to our old and various favourites,
which sometimes, of course, belonged to that exalted trio.

So, to the South Western: Great was the beauty of the
annual pilgrimage into Wessex! There was that scramble about

the old Waterloo. What a place! Back in the eighteen-fifties it had possessed only three platforms, but then, and to the bitter last, added to the platform lines was a through road to the South Eastern at Waterloo Junction, bisecting the South Western station on what was theoretically a level crossing. It was not really so; the platform surface gave a dip to the tracks, like a hump-back bridge in reverse, and there was a pedestrian drawbridge as well. The extension, called the Windsor station, was added in 1860; in 1879 there appeared the South station, with a single island platform, and always known as Cyprus, after a protectorate newly acquired in the year of its birth. Another odd piece, called Khartoum, was stuck on the Windsor Station in 1885, and thus, with sixteen platforms, Waterloo had grown up into that labyrinth of shabby sheds and dreary halls, horrifying to a stranger yet delectable to a boy, which became London's best practical joke.

Neither authors nor editors could leave it alone. Jerome K. Jerome dragged it into *Three Men in a Boat* and gave it a "high level" platform which was about the one thing it did not possess. W. J. Locke made the kind, correct, and sorely misjudged Marcus Ordeyne drink an improbable pot of beer in it, and at the time of the Entente Cordiale in 1904, *Punch* announced that it was to be presented to France as a token of esteem and regard, and that the French Government was going to re-erect it in the Champs Élysées. But at long last the London and South Western very properly began to rebuild it. Gradually and gauntly, a new landmark grew into the Lambeth skyline, at first where Cyprus had formerly been. The old place died hard. Not until 1922, the last year of the South Western's life, was the new station completed, with twenty-one platforms instead of the originally intended twenty-three. Even now, Waterloo contains a bit of old Khartoum on the Windsor side. Platform twenty-one is the old sixteen.

But the old station was inimitable. The rambling battered caravanserai of London Bridge, seared and gutted by fire bombs, is yet simplicity itself compared with the old Waterloo. Waterloo's "A" signalbox, straddling the bottleneck outside, was, we were told, the largest in the world. Built in 1892, it had 248 levers before reconstruction, and was plumed by a magnificent array of route-indicating signals. For many years Waterloo also had one of the smallest signalboxes. This was the Crowsnest, a queer little cabin up a pole, dating from the days when incoming trains had been slipped altogether by their engines. The locomotive used to put on a spurt after slipping. While it ran forward into a siding, by a masterpiece of juggling, the points were altered between the tender and the leading coach, so that the train overtook its own engine and trundled solemnly into the station by itself. That is ancient history; the Waterloo most of us knew was the monstrous conglomeration of the nineteen hundreds.

There was something very magnificent about the L.S.W.R. West of England express. It was much better than any ordinary train on other lines originating south of the Thames, for unlike its southern neighbours, the South Western took corridor trains seriously from the beginning of the century. In the middle was a dining car that advertised its presence by a clerestory roof considerably higher than anything else. The colour scheme was without parallel. While the upper panels were officially described as "salmon," and were rather like tinned salmon when quite new, they weathered into a terra-cotta brown after about a week. But to us, who knew and loved the South-Western, it was above criticism. There was splendour even in the bright brass handrails inside corridor windows; the first-class carriages with their blue broadcloth and profusion of gold lace, even on the window straps and slings, were truly gorgeous, the brown plush seconds, which, like the firsts, could be identified from afar by their lemon-yellow window frames, were admirable, and the thirds, though dowdy, were solidly comfortable.

There at the head of the train was one of Dugald Drummond's express engines. No locomotive was more beautiful than a Drummond T 9 four-coupled in her glory of light green and rich lining-out. A thin film of clean grease covered her and was worked into a fascinating pattern that showed up in the sun like a watermark. Her brass safety-valve columns glittered, delicately as the crown of a Swedish bride, on her small shapely dome. She was a lovely thing!

Away we went, out into the green fields, which began at Raynes Park, through the heath of West Surrey, into Hampshire and past Farnborough with its prodigious new airship shed. More mysterious even than the anxious-looking airship which, on a red-letter day, might be butting into the wind overhead, was the line which here passed over ours at right-angles. It had odd signals with a round white spot on the red, and was, most surprisingly to uninformed youth, the Reading branch of the South Eastern and Chatham.

Then came Basingstoke and the Great Western, regarded as a quaint and exotic next-door neighbour, and then the rolling chalk. At Whitchurch was another of those mysterious lines crossing underneath. It was the Didcot, Newbury, and Southampton. At a remote age I painted a highly imaginative picture of a D.N. and S. train; I never forgave the line for turning out to be for all practical purposes, a branch of the Great Western after all! And so to Andover Junction. Now Andover was a very remarkable place indeed; it was the southern terminus of the Midland and South Western Junction Railway, of which the other extremity, improbably but truly, was Andoversford in the Cotswolds.

This was a small railway, with a poverty-stricken history, but under Sam Fay it had nevertheless grown into a model line from the passengers' point of view. It gave that rare thing, a really good cross-country service, for which, for better or worse, we nowadays seek rather in motor coaching circles. Cheltenham, where the M.S.W.J. terminated by virtue of running powers, had of course a main-line through service from Paddington. But if you chose your trains, travelling from Waterloo to Andover, and thence took the M.S.W.J. North Express, you could get to Cheltenham more quickly than by the Great Western with its wanderings round by Gloucester.

The Midland and South Western Junction trains were red, like those of the Midland, though it was a wholly independent line. Unlike those of the Midland, or the Great Western, or the

South Western, its carriages all had electric light in its latter days, even the horseboxes, and Tyrrell's express engines, very neat, with the company's initials in flowery copperplate script on the tenders, were as good as those of many bigger companies. A great little railway! When the Great Western engulfed it in 1923, the result was not an improvement.

Beyond Andover, a new magic came into those long-ago journeys. We had entered Wessex, and something older than Wessex; the mysterious Plain was about us as we raced along high embankment or white chalky cutting. As Grateley flashed past, close to the railway there was a hill with a Celtic fort on the summit; somewhere out on the Plain beyond the lonely Amesbury branch was Stonehenge—we called it simply The Stones— unmarred by gaunt hangar or mean hutment; as yet unprofaned by the heedless Motoring Many.

Then there was Tunnel Junction, with Sarum's spire showing over the skyline; there was the tunnel itself, followed by the violent reverse curves into Salisbury station. A little while before, the station curve had been the scene of one of the South Western's few major tragedies; of that, more later. The little boy who was I saw and remembered another railway accident at Salisbury, a very jolly one for the heartless onlooker.

The principal actors were a porter and an Adams 0–4–2 Jubilee engine. The porter was pushing a trolley, piled high with luggage, over the crossing at the eastern end of the station; the Jubilee was drifting in with the awful stealth of the light engine. Just when he had pushed the trolley so far, the porter saw the Jubilee. He was human. He fled.

Then the Jubilee took the trolley amidships. With one brief crunch it was gone. A buffer punched sweetly into a great trunk, a tuckbox exploded, a holdall ceased to hold and laid all before us. Neat suits, good jams and choice preserves, dainty millinery and masculine high boots rose in swarm from that riven hive. Into the station careered a vision of the *Jubilee Adorned*. A big picture hat crowned a lamp-iron; snowy lingerie blossomed in strange places, or danced a delicate rigadoon on a coupling rod.

There was a final tortured scream of brakes and wreckage in

chorus, then all was still. Strong men, brows bent in horror, leaped down into that vale of tears and began to cram soiled and scattered finery back into split portmanteaux and scalped bandboxes. It was a great destruction. Doubtless much more followed, but at that point a Great Western train came clanking in. I had never before seen a locomotive with double frames and with so immense a brass dome, nor yet a train of carriages completely clerestoried. I turned my back on my first railway accident. Forgive me, reader, for I was only five!

Salisbury was where we left the express. With a fresh engine it disappeared into the unknown West. Later days brought experience of crimson Devon earth, of the magnificent climb from Seaton Junction to Honiton Tunnel, of the two Exeters, of Dartmoor and the great Meldon Viaduct, and of remote Padstow, a sort of railway Hy Brasil beyond the sunset. As yet we were for the local train, an amiable caravan serving all stations to Exeter, a train that should pause at Milborne Port, linger by Sherborne and dally with Sutton Bingham and Crewkerne, places which the express ignored save maybe to yell at their distant signals. Our local sat all leisurely in the bay until the express had cleared Wilton. A friendly train; its engine might be anything from a four-cylinder 4–6–0 (not Mr. Drummond's most sparkling work) to an Adams veteran of the early 'eighties; its carriages had the faded gentility of an early Victorian parlour in the deep country, for there was buff velveteen in the first class and a delicious smell about it.

Where the express had raced, the local ambled; where the express had played something like Schumann's *Arabesque* on the railjoints, the local played a gentle pavane. It gave you time to study the outline of Wilton's great Italianesque church, the thatched roofs of Barford St. Martin, the solemn line of the Downs and the lovely, lovely valley of the Nadder. And when at last we left it, there would be the same pony-trap with the same brown mare, the same ride to the same three-centuries-old house with the pomegranate tree on the south wall. There the trains were invisible, but if you woke in the small hours you had their occasional distant roar on the other side of the ridge for

16

Andover Locomotive Sidings, 1910: Adams' seven-footer No. 446 (Drummond boiler) built in 1883 for the London and South Western Railway, and Dübs 4-4-0 No. 9, Midland and South Western Junction Railway in 1893. Both engines originally had plain chimneys, as shown in right background. In left background is part of a South Western bogie coach of 1882

company, and in the daytime there was a glorious occupation crossing only half a mile away. On that crossing I learnt to flatten farthings into ha'pennies; there I learnt, without giving it a name, to recognize a Drummond T 9 as the most beautiful of engines at the age of two years and two months.

That was my journey on the London and South Western. Substitute for the grace of the Drummond engine the pride of a Claud Hamilton on the Great Eastern or the royal magnificence of a Johnson single on the Midland, or whatever; ring changes on the Cumbrian fells, the Welsh Marches, or where you will, and you have the rare delight of your own first journeyings. A smell encountered thirty years after can bring them back; so can noises, a few bars of music, certain lights on certain hills, or the spectacle of an ancient locomotive on a branch line.

Eighteen-seventy-four begins our period. In January of that year the first British Pullman cars were being assembled from American-built parts in the Midland Railway works at Derby. For the Midland, too, the first ordinary bogie carriages were being built. Stroudley on the London, Brighton and South Coast had lately inaugurated a school of locomotive design and a policy of standardization which were to be models to the world. The British train, having emerged from the archaic, was timidly assuming the form in which it was to be known for several generations. Six years before, the Midland Railway had reached London; two years on, the Midland route to Scotland would be completed, the last of the great Anglo-Scottish trunk lines.

Imagine, then, St. Pancras on an early summer night of 1876! The place is familiar even to visitors out of the future. Gilbert Scott's façade of proud and shameless Victorian Gothic, and Barlow's incomparable roof, are just eight years old; nobody guesses what blows will some day strike them from the unimagined air, or how they will survive those blows. No, this is the summer of 1876 and the Settle and Carlisle line has been open for all traffic since May Day. It is really an admirable thing, this new Midland Scotch express. Euston and King's Cross have their eyes on it, for it is a much finer train than anything the North Western or the Great Northern can show as yet. The Midland, moreover, is competing with both; partnership with the Glasgow and South Western—the wee Sou'-West which nobody else in England took seriously—is getting Midland trains into Glasgow, while the North British has joyously double-crossed its East Coast allies and is running Midland expresses into Edinburgh by the Waverley route.

There in St. Pancras stands the superb line of carriages; a twelve-wheel composite, some six-wheelers—even these very superior of their kind—and a Pullman sleeping car for Edinburgh. What a Pullman, at that! The full exuberance of American decorative art of the President Grant era blossoms inside and out. The name, *Castalia*, glitters in an oval-framed scroll on each side, amid a welter of panels gorgeous in gold-leaf on a dark-brown base.

Tragic *Castalia!* Fated soon to be transferred by the Pullman Company to the Continent, eight years hence on an Italian November night she will be burnt down to the axles. But on this summer evening of 1876, terribly new and unblemished, she furnishes sleeping accommodation for the *best people*. She scintillates with silverplate and gilding, her handsome bronze kerosene lamps gleam in a coloured clerestory, shedding a warm radiance over rich panels and sleek plush. There, in a little while, stately gentlemen will be cautiously extracting themselves from broadcloth and starch, fine ladies and lovely girls will be shedding stiff linen and whalebone as delicately as possible within the uneasy privacy of their green-curtained berths— save for the plutocrats who have booked the single private compartment at the end. Here, under the vast, dim parabola of roof, we see only the dignity, the elegance, the last word in travelling comfort to be spoken in the mid-'seventies.

Farther down there is another Pullman, and more coaches, crimson Midlands and one or two green Glasgow and South Westerns, bound for the Clyde. At the head, superbly in tandem, are two of Matthew Kirtley's latest and finest express engines, deep emerald green and so clean that they reflect the station and signal lamps as if theirs were a vitreous rather than a ferrous quality. Midland engines are unexcelled in their cleanliness and the beauty of their finish. Only Stroudley's yellow engines on the London, Brighton and South Coast really rival them.

If we make this journey in the Pullman car, we shall have comfortable beds—once we have managed to get properly into them. In an ordinary carriage, however, we shall see more of the journey, and unless the August rush be on, still travel in reasonable comfort. The Midland twelve-wheeler of the 'seventies is much loftier than its rivals, matching thus the Pullman car, and its oaken bogies run most gently. Its weak points, compared with the carriages of years to come, are the poor lamps, a winter dependence on footwarmers, and a lack of lavatories, which last only the Pullman cars possess. Subject, therefore, to a warm summer night, a disinclination to read, and a careful personal timetable, one may travel well in it. The first-class seats are admirable; the thirds—for the Midland abolished second-class a year before—are quite spacious and decently upholstered, which qualities are more than one finds on any rival railways as yet.

Our departure is slow but easy; the gasworks, stark against the lurid London night sky, drifts by on the right and we are off past Kentish Town and its steam sheds with a tranquillity lacking in the North Western's vociferous climb to Chalk Farm or the Great Northern's sulphurous and slippery toiling up to Finsbury Park. Here on the Midland, the syncopated double-exhaust of the two Kirtley 2–4–0's settles down sweetly to the long soft roar of engines running at speed. With West Hampstead the suburbs pass away into our wake; the train soon rolls northwards through the darkness of the deep country.

Bedford and Kettering are but dim oases in a desert of darkness, but the Midlands bring iron and steel, and in this year of 'seventy-six no futuristic notions of fuel economy muzzle the furnaces. With ineffable pride the flames leap to the skies; boldly ruddy float the clouds over Sheffield and through the midst glides our Midland express, a duskily luminous serpent at home in her native Pandemonium.

And so, in the small, small hours, we come to Normanton, a most important place. By day the great expresses solemnly wait here while the passengers sit down to one of the best, and certainly one of the most quickly served luncheons or dinners in England. The other two are at York on the North Eastern and Preston on the North Western. At all three there are magnificent dining rooms where you may sit down in comfort and dignity, eat and drink with steady deliberation for half-an-hour, and go on your way.

But on the night train a short drink and a supper basket are best. Each has his various taste and capacity, and you may choose anything from champagne to two-penn'orth of whisky. Few things are nicer than a cold chicken, eaten in a railway carriage on the far side of midnight. Such meals, and shut windows, form the sovereign soporific, the sure preventative of the early morning chill and queasy lassitude which beset the inexperienced.

At last the fiery lands are left behind. Leeds is in our rear and the train has reversed. Two fresh engines, with smaller coupled wheels, face the long hike over the fells.

The older Midland route to the North, for what it was worth, existed by virtue of the North-Western Railway (not the London and North Western, observe, but what was known as the Little North-Western), between Skipton and Morecambe via Hellifield and Lancaster. The Midland made a working agreement with the Little N.W.R. in 1852, leased it in 1859 and bought it in 1871, gaining thereby a tap on the London and North Western at Lancaster. North of Lancaster, naturally, the London and North Western had the road and very much of its own way. It is over the erstwhile Little North-Western that we now pass to Hellifield, leaving it before that remote and improbable Clapham Junction that is to be found on the flank of the Pennines. At Settle Junction, a few miles north-west of Hellifield, the new line begins. Noisily, with the twin pillar of fire at our head, we climb up the valley of the Ribble, between the black masses of Ingleboro' and Pen-y-Ghent, with Whernside somewhere in the darkness ahead of us.

This line, since the first sod was cut at Anley in 1869, has been a roaring trail of shanty towns. Here the old English navvy, whose race will pass with the nineteenth century, has plied his pick, tipped his barrow, smashed the face of his enemy, sported his fancy waistcoat of a Sunday, lost it and everything else save his shirt, breeches and boots at crown-and-anchor on Monday night, and fallen to afresh on the last great main line to the Border, every week of the five and a half years between November of 1869 and the summer of 1875.

For thirteen miles from Settle, we climb steadily up the long scarcely broken stretches at 1 in 100. Pen-y-Ghent's dead volcano is behind us; with a great shout the train plunges into Blea Moor Tunnel and the massive shoulder of Whernside. A mighty work, that tunnel, carried out with the primitive tools of the time, a monument to Sharland, the Tasmanian engineer who built the Settle and Carlisle line. There are seven shafts; from these and from the two extremities, sixteen faces were tackled at once during construction. Thereafter, past Hawes Junction,* we roar along the high places of the Backbone of England, the great hills still black against the pale light of dawn, the whole dim scene inexpressibly gaunt and terrific, severe and aloof from the new railway that gashes its face. A window cautiously lowered for an instant lets in a wind like a whiplash. Rearward the volute clouds of the exhaust hang, unevaporated, as a vast floating cable of whitey-grey for miles back along the curves we have traversed.

From Blea Moor on to Ais Gill, where the line reaches its summit level of 1,169 feet, is eleven miles, and then to Carlisle it is forty-eight miles. Ais Gill is on the watershed; one way flows the Ure through Wensleydale to Ripon and the Plain of York, the other way flows the Eden which we shall follow to the end of England. Swinging down by Hell Gill and the bleak table-mountain of Wild Boar Fell, the strange new song of the bogie carriages quickens its beat; with joyous cries to one another the engines begin to sprint on the last stretch of their journey.

What a place is Carlisle! Far more of a frontier than that

* Now Garsdale.

border junction which will be known to later generations. Now, in the grey early morning, it roars with the life of high noon; cans and barrows rumble back and forth; men call out eerily in the mist drifting from Solway. The refreshment rooms are doing a roaring trade, and so, after their kind, are the lavatories. This is the end of the two longest railways in England. There is a black Jumbo off the London and North Western; not the glum, dirty black engine of years to come but a beautiful glistening thing; somebody has called the colour blackberry black, and this is rather a good description. It was Francis Webb of the London and North Western who said he was prepared to paint his engines any colour the directors liked so long as it was black. The story is fated to become a chestnut; years after, people will tell it anew about Henry Ford.

Over there on the east side is one of Fletcher's engines on the North Eastern, severe and Quakerish of outline, but painted bright green. Her driver has further embellished her with a pair of polished-brass antlered stags on her uncompromising stove-pipe chimney and there is a gaudy transfer picture of the Royal Family on her sandbox. Those pictures are all the rage among North Eastern enginemen just now and old Father Fletcher has no objection so long as the engines are kept clean and do not break down. There is destined to be trouble about it later on, nevertheless, when a picture of *Venus Asleep* (or is it Goya's *Duchess Undraped?*) goes to York on a North Eastern sandbox and attracts the scandalized attention of a very important dignitary.

The old N.E.R. Quaker has come across from Newcastle. In contradistinction to her enormous bellmouth dome, there is one of Jimmy Stirling's magnificent Glasgow and South Western bogie seven-footers with a domeless boiler—a clean sweep from the massive muzzle-loader chimney to the Ramsbottom safety-valves at the back, and the little engine that has brought in the milk off the Maryport and Carlisle line is domeless also. With the exception of the black North Western Jumbo, all these locomotives are arrayed in various shades of the conventional engine green. But on the two largest Scottish lines, whose territory marches with that of their allies at Carlisle, things are far otherwise. The Caledonian engines, though unimposing in size (all legs and wings, according to Dugald Drummond), are magnificently accoutred in royal blue, and now, at the head of our Edinburgh Pullman, resplendent in mustard yellow and claret, stands one of the most superb, most puissant and most advanced locomotives in Europe.

North British express engine No. 479, *Abbotsford*, designed by the young but already autocratic Drummond, is one of a quartet, newly and specially built for the Midland Scotch expresses over the Waverley route. The others are Nos. 476–478, *Carlisle*, *Edinburgh* and *Melrose*. A 4–4–0 bogie engine, with inside cylinders, she and her three sisters, to which eight more will be added in the next two years, are the direct ancestresses of hundreds of locomotives, gradually increasing in size but all true to the basic Drummond design. Dugald Drummond will take it, and enlarge upon it, on the Caledonian and the London and South Western. His brother, Peter Drummond, will do likewise on the Highland and the Glasgow and South Western. Matthew Holmes and Willie Reid will perpetuate it, in larger engines, on the North British, culminating in the beautiful Glens and Scotts of the early twentieth century. On the Caledonian, J. Lambie and J. F. McIntosh will do likewise, producing locomotives which will be responsible, in their time, for the fastest express running in Great Britain.

Viewed dispassionately, Drummond's new express engine is in many respects an enlargement of Stroudley's design for the London, Brighton and South Coast, with a pair of after-coupled wheels and a leading bogie added. The cylinders and motion are the same, and so, in all main features, is the boiler. The astonishing yellow livery is "Stroudley's improved engine green," in truth a dark orange ochre with an invisible seasoning of bronze green. Its inventor first used it on the Highland Railway in the 'sixties before taking it to Brighton. At Brighton, Drummond was Stroudley's works manager before coming north to the North British Railway and bringing the "green" back to Scotland with him. Long years after, sentimentalists, talking about the Brighton and the North British, but particularly about the Brighton, will enthuse about "canary-coloured locomotives," or even "their bright livery of daffodil yellow." It is nothing of the kind; in shadow it is nearest to fresh French mustard; in sunshine it takes on a lovely lustre like that of old yellow majolica.

On the stroke of five o'clock, with the sun rising out of the mist on the Border hills, *Abbotsford* pulls out of Carlisle with the night Pullman. No double-heading here; though the train is heavy, burdened with through carriages from various parts of the Midlands and West of England as well as the coaches and the Pullman from London, she faces the long, sinuous switch back through the Border counties alone. For the 45½ miles to Hawick, including the eight mile climb at 1 in 75 from Newcastleton to Whitrope, she is allowed 68 minutes. The day Pullman has four minutes knocked off, but may be allowed a banking engine from Newcastleton.

Over the Border mosses goes the Waverley Route Pullman, the big Drummond engine getting away from Carlisle with a smartness and easy competence that are an object lesson to many railways held in higher esteem than the North British, and through Liddesdale into Scotland; as the morning sun grows stronger on the great bare slopes of Roan Fell and his neighbours, imagination plays with the rhythm of the bogies over the railjoints, easily setting to their song the old ranting ballad of *Lock the door, Lariston!* From Newcastleton the climbing begins in earnest and we watch that glorious yellow engine, in the full pride of her beauty now that the sun strikes her, pounding round the great curves that bring us to the summit. Then there is the lovely gallop down to Hawick, our first stop in Scotland, where the morning smokes rise in straight plumes from the grey mill town among the hills. In the locomotive yard there is one of the North British company's antiques, still with the bright green livery of Drummond's predecessor, Tom Wheatley, and sporting a plain chimney, like a North Eastern engine. Mr. Wheatley has gone farther west to take a lease of the Wigtownshire Railway and to work it (gorgeous idea!) as a private family business. The North British Railway is still burdened with a fantastic collection of ancient locomotives, some of them dating back to the 'forties; of its ordinary trains, the standard of their punctuality and the quality of their carriages, the less said the better. But its Pullman trains over the Waverley Route nevertheless exhibit some of the finest running in the world, over such a line.

So we come to Newtown St. Boswells (the North British drops the Newtown, although the old town is a good tramp away across country), and then, nestling below the calm peaks of the Eildons, those great little mountains that, once seen in youth, can never be forgotten, there is Melrose, very Presbyterian, douce and demure as a Scots lass in grey tweed. People are sitting down to breakfast in Melrose; the station is quite lively. The train decants several London Scots and their families returning to make holiday with their own people; out of the Pullman car comes a prosperous American poppa with his lady and his progeny, all ready to do the Scott country.

Between Melrose and Galashiels we cross the Tweed, then we follow Gala Water before reaching the second summit of the line at Falahill. From the summit, for eight miles, there is a downhill stretch with a ruling and almost continuous gradient of 1 in 70. In spite of having this against it, the best up train covers the $33\frac{1}{2}$ miles from Edinburgh to Galashiels in 52 minutes. Five years on, in 1881, the night Pullmans, hauled by the same engines, will be doing even better work, with non-stop runs in each direction between Carlisle and Edinburgh at a 42 mile-an-hour average.

From Falahill it is easy going down into the Lothians; the bogie engine and carriages take the curves with an absence of bumps rare on other railways, even on the London and North Western, which, while it prides itself on the best permanent way in the world, will have nothing to do with bogies, now or for many years to come. Collieries rear their unkempt headgear about Gorebridge before we join the East Coast Route and run in over the last stretch to the Scottish capital.

Even now, our final approach is at a spanking pace; none of the long, cautious crawl which distinguishes trains without continuous brakes. In the last minutes only, during the smoky passage of the Calton Hill tunnel, is there a long sigh from the Westinghouse air installation and a shudder passing through the train as the automatic brakes do their work. Dunedin's ten-storey lands soar after their own morning reek, with the sunshine gilding the Salisbury Craigs beyond, as we slip in at last to the shabby labyrinth that is the Waverley Station of eighteen-seventy-six.

\*     \*     \*

Let not the reader dismiss this as retrospect through rosy glasses. Those were delectable journeys, but many were not; certainly in the 'seventies and even in the nineteen-hundreds. There were few things in British passenger transport poorer than a South Eastern third-class suburban carriage; a North London third was, perhaps, one of them. There were few trains, of main-line status, more squalid in these islands than an ordinary North British train calling at all stations from Edinburgh to Glasgow, few places meaner than the older London and South Western stations, and most of them were old. Wimbledon, Dorchester, Exeter Queen Street, they were alike deplorable, though there was at least unconscious humour about Dorchester, where the down trains stopped at a ramshackle platform outside the station and the through up trains from Weymouth had to overshoot it and back in after stopping on the London side (they still do); but we, who loved trains, forgave much. Even the doddering conduct of all Great Western services except the show-pieces failed to sully the charm of those local trains that ambled in at last with two or three rabbits, and perhaps a pheasant, hanging up in a dark corner of the cab. On many lines, enginemen and signalmen used to have a gentlemen's agreement regarding the collection and allocation of game knocked down by the trains. Nowadays, most lines have either too many trains to make this workable, or else none at all, but it is nice, and not unreasonable, to suppose that it still goes on in the place I have in mind, and in other places where one engine in steam serves some remote branch of a branch.

26

# CHAPTER TWO

# THE OLD COMPANIES

## *London's Railways*

THE *London and North Western Railway is noted for Punctuality, Speed, Smooth Riding, Dustless Tracks, Safety and Comfort, and is the Oldest Established Firm in the Railway Passenger Business.*

To an Edwardian railway amateur those lines, quoted on the backs of many thousands of admirable picture post-cards published by the North Western between the close of the South African war and the beginning of the Kaiser's, could scarcely be disputed in mixed company. The North Western, as already remarked, was the Premier Line. There were very occasional attempts to apply this title to the Great Western, usually by people who knew the Cornish Riviera Limited better than they knew the Cornish branch lines; the London and South Western assumed the title of the Royal Road, by joint virtue of Windsor and the Isle of Wight, but the fact remained, whether you liked it or not, that the North Western *was* the Premier Line. To dispute it was in as bad taste as to introduce religious or political controversy to the conversation at one of the Vicar's tea parties.

The North Western was noted for its punctuality, just as the Highland was not. In speed its general standard was high, though at various times there were faster regular trains on the Great Central, the North Eastern, and the Caledonian. The Midland, too, won on points when it came to the largest number of smartly-timed trains between cities. The claim to smooth riding was undeniable. You might look at a North Western carriage, and its suspension seemed just like that of another company's, yet somehow it had the ability to drift along as if it were skimming an oil film at a mile a minute. It was helped,

27

of course, by a standard of permanent way second to none in the world. The sonorous *duddidy-dun—duddidy-dun—duddidy-dun\** of North Western rolling stock travelling at speed was heard but not felt. Those magnificent tracks were famous for their dustless quality because, at an early date when there was little or nothing but sand in the ballast used by some companies, the North Western would regard only the best granite chips. The safety claim was justified, but so it was for all the British main lines. There was ill-luck at times—the unexplained disasters at Shrewsbury, Salisbury and Grantham were the collective burden of the North Western, the South Western, and the Great Northern—but one sought far among British railway accidents for the disgraceful circumstances of careless and reckless working which distinguished many American railways right up to the nineteen-hundreds.

In spite of a number of ancient stations in important places, the North Western looked good. Those pale buff-coloured stations were cleaner and neater than other stations; they were often architecturally interesting, from the Regency classicism of the original London to Birmingham series to the Victorian neo-Tudor of the Trent Valley line. To this day, too, an interesting diversion while travelling up the old North Western main line is to observe the occasional farmhouses built by the North Western, in one of its several successive architectural styles, to accommodate those displaced when the line was first built. North Western engines were not the most beautiful in the world, and the trains often exhibited a quaint up-and-downness in respect of carriage roofs, yet a North Western express had great dignity. The old 2.0 p.m. Scotch Express, the Corridor, likewise the American boat specials put on between Liverpool and Euston in 1907, were beauties.

The immense variety of the engine names caught everybody's fancy—*Charles Dickens, Harlequin, Psyche, Courier, Sunbeam, George the Fifth, Superb, Sister Dora*—they were alike delightful. I was a little puzzled by *Sister Dora*, though; for one thing, she was a quite unsisterly-looking Jumbo, and secondly she did not

* Acknowledgement to Edmund Vale:

originally have that name at all. She was formerly named *Serpent*. Many of the names were handed down from engine to engine. The first *Courier* was a Crampton's patent 4–2–0 built by Alexander Allan at Crewe in 1847. The last *Courier* was a Jumbo, built by Webb in 1877 and rebuilt in 1896; one of her handsome brass nameplates adorns my dining-room chimney-piece.

There remains one claim on the North Western's blurb to be considered. It called itself the *Oldest Established Firm in the Railway Passenger Business*. Passing over the quibble of whether a statutory company is a firm, we must still regard that claim as something of a commercial prevarication. The London and North Western Railway was formed by amalgamation in 1846. It was therefore considerably younger than the Great Western and the London and South Western, to mention only main lines radiating from London. The basis of its claim was the fact that the Liverpool and Manchester, a constituent of one of its constituents, was the first railway to convey passengers by regular services with steam locomotive traction. There was not enough space on the backs of the post-cards to explain all that. The rightful claimant to the title as stated was the Swansea and Mumbles Railway in South Wales, incorporated as the Oystermouth Railway or Tramroad Company in 1804.

The London and North Western Railway owed its eminence and respectability not only to geographical and economic factors; it had a series of great men on both its business and its engineering sides. Two contemporary giants were Richard Moon and Francis Webb. Moon was chairman of the North Western from 1861 to 1891. Contemporary portraiture shows us a face severe to the point of caricature with its cold, hard eyes below rocky brows, its knife-thin mouth below a deep upper lip, its steeply angular lines under the cheeks. Under Sir Richard Moon, as he became, the London and North Western grew from a hotchpotch of half-assimilated lesser undertakings, for old traditions lingered long after the amalgamation of 1846, to one of the largest, wealthiest and most respected joint-stock corporations in the world. Irreverent stories about Moon only confirm his reputation. If it was not a general manager, it was certainly someone very high-up who, entering the general offices at 9.4 a.m., was greeted thus by the chairman one day: "Good morning, sir! The North Western hours are nine till six." The terrible tale of what happened to the clerk who turned up at Euston one Saturday morning, wearing flannel trousers, was told with bated breath for years after, and there was a legend at Euston to the effect that pigeons had ceased to frequent the station ever since the fatal morning when one bird had made an unfortunate error of judgment just as Sir Richard was on his way to the board room in a new silk hat.

Francis Webb was chief mechanical engineer from 1871 to 1903. Here again was severe autocracy personified, yet Moon and Webb continued harmoniously in power through all those years. Webb is even reputed to have courted Moon's daughter, but apparently Miss Moon had other notions, and thereafter Webb devoted his entire life to the mechanical side of the North Western, a cold, harsh, lonely man considering no ideas but his own, fecund in his original inventiveness, instant as cordite to take offence, intolerant of his subordinates and icily munificent in the great causes of Victorian charity. That Moon and Webb got on together seems to have been due to Moon's giving the head of Crewe *carte-blanche* to manage his department as he thought fit, without interference. The duties of Moon's general manager must have been arduous indeed, and fully testing to the great diplomatic gifts of William Cawkwell and Sir George Findlay.

So there was the London and North Western, the Premier Line of England, with a total route mileage of 2,009, worked by 3,068 locomotives, extending northwards from London to Carlisle, and westwards to Ireland, whither the company operated steamer services and where it owned the Dundalk, Newry and Greenore Railway.*

Turning eastwards along the Euston Road brought us to St. Pancras and to the Midland, about which I have made several observations already. Two claims could be made safely

* These and following similar statistics are taken from the 1914 returns.

for the Midland Railway. It had the best stations in England and the most comfortable third-class carriages in the world. The company believed in lightly-loaded expresses. There were frequent fast services, and some of them contrived to be very fast in spite of a peculiar undersizedness of its locomotives. During our period, and indeed to the end of its separate existence, the Midland had no six-coupled express engines. The latter-day Midland Scotch express ran from St. Pancras to Leeds behind a small 4–4–0 three-cylinder compound with Deeley's modification of the Smith system of compounding. Beyond Leeds this would usually be replaced by one of Deeley's 999 class, which was the same engine with two simple-expansion inside cylinders substituted for the compound arrangement. The compounds—the standard Midland express engine to the last, and becoming, in a slightly modified form, the standard L.M.S. express engine for several years in the nineteen-twenties —were designed in 1905 and in their turn had been modified from the Smith system compounds designed by S. W. Johnson in 1901. Likewise the Midland goods traffic; all down the years the great coal trains from Yorkshire to London plodded solemnly along their separate tracks behind small, and often ancient 0–6–0 locomotives working in pairs. Still, the Midland managed without breakdown or disrepute, indeed, it was a railway which stood very highly in the public favour.

The quality of Midland stations was due, at least in part, to the fact that as railways went the Midland was a very warm company and could afford to be unstinting. The excellence of the carriages was the joint result of the benevolence shown towards third-class passengers by James Allport as general manager, and of the sympathetic skill of Tom Clayton and David Bain, successive carriage superintendents. In the early 'eighties, S. W. Johnson, Kirtley's successor at the head of the Locomotive Department, began to paint his engines red, matching the coaches. Roger Fry, yearning as a boy after beauty and colour in a sepia-toned Quaker household, gazed on the poppies in his father's North London garden, dreamed about locomotives, and told himself that somewhere, some-when, he would see a *pure red engine*. That, I believe, was before the Midland shed its original green livery. True, in earlier days, several lines had gone in for a rather flat Indian red, the London and South Western up to 1859 and the old Southern Division of the London and North Western prior to 1861. But what the young Fry was really hankering for was something like the North Western's *Greater Britain* which, at the time of the 1897 Jubilee, was painted vermilion. At the same time, the L.N.W.R. *Queen Empress* was painted white, the notion being that, as Caledonian engines were blue anyway, the Queen's motive power on her summer journey to Balmoral would be suitably patriotic in hue.

The Midland train best remembered was an all-over crimson from end to end, set off by black and yellow lines, and prefixed by a vermilion buffer-beam on the engine, embellished, not with the conventional number but with the proud initials M.R. The London Midland and Scottish inherited this colour scheme in 1923, but as the years advanced the red seemed to lose some of its quality, the ruby lacked its old lustre somehow, then vanished altogether from all but the carriages and the most modern express engines, and finally gave way to the present disgusting dowdiness of slate black and dreary maroon.

Midland trains looked at their finest just at the turn of the century. S. W. Johnson was locomotive superintendent and his engines were things of beauty. One of his bogie single-drivers, crowned by its original, inimitable chimney, hauling a train of Clayton's last design of main-line passenger stock, was a superb sight, whether it were threading the spectacular Derbyshire dales or racing through the tamely pleasant hunting country of the South Midlands. Clayton's carriages showed artistry in little things. In his final designs, as in Bain's, which followed, the end panels were continuous, that is to say there was no break in the middle ones where they cleared the level of the lower decks on each side and entered that of the clerestory. Consequently, the clerestory itself seemed to grow out of the carriage body, whereas, on other lines using this form of roof, it looked at the ends as if the coach had been built first and the

Down Midland express hauled by Johnson large 4-4-0 locomotive No. 767, with tender of No. 761. The first four vehicles are: Clayton third class of the late 'eighties; Clayton saloon of the late 'nineties. Clayton diner of 1892 and a Bain brake third (*circa* 1910)

[*F. Moore's Railway Photographs*]

Coal and Marguerites: Characteristic view of a rebuilt Kirtley goods engine at work
on the Midland Railway

*[Locomotive and General Railway Photographs]*

Midland express of the 'seventies: Kirtley's 2–4–0 No. 1086, as originally built,
with one of Clayton's earliest bogie coaches

*[Locomotive and General Railway Photographs]*

The Native Compound: R. M. Deeley's No. 1008 hauling a Midland express, about 1910

[*L.M.S.R. Records*]

*Vesuvius* in eruption: Webb Dreadnought class three-cylinder compound passing over Bushey Troughs with up Belfast boat train, London and North Western Railway

[*T. F. Budden*]

Carlisle at the turn of the century: Up West Coast express headed by a Black Prince class four-cylinder Webb compound and piloted by 2–4–0 No. 39 *Thalaba*; in left background is a shunting Midland train

One of Bowen-Cooke's famous George the Fifth class on an up express near Kenton, London and North Western Railway. A post-1914 view (see conductor rails in foreground)

[*E. Mason, Railway Photographs*]

Down Great Northern express, about 45 years ago, near Hadley Wood, drawn by
two Stirling eight-footers. This is a spectacle that would have caused a memorable
row in Patrick Stirling's lifetime

[*T. F. Budden*]

Up Scotsman passing Low Fell, North Eastern Railway, in 1882, hauled by
Fletcher 2–4–0 express engine No. 153

[*F. Moore's Railway Photographs*]

H. A. Ivatt's Atlantic
No. 1447 on a down
Great Northern ex
press; the large leading
carriage was of a type
usually employed or
the Leeds expresses

[*F. Moore's
Railway Photographs*]

clerestory stuck on afterwards, an operation which the London and South Western actually carried out in 1887 on a royal saloon built in 1885. Aesthetically, the Midland arrangement was the only satisfactory one for a square-ended clerestory, which otherwise could not compare for appearance with the domed end used on Pullman cars and on the best Great Northern and East Coast Joint stock.

The comfort of the Midland carriages has already been remarked. You felt, in a Midland third class, that the company really did regard you as being as important as your first-class neighbours. There was a very Victorian style of decoration, with its quasi-Persian pattern on a yellow ground in the handsome moquette squabs, its flowery white lincrusta panels on the ceilings, suggestive in their richest form of whitewashed fruit salad, its frilled opal-glass shades to the lamps in those carriages which had advanced to electric light, its heavily carved mouldings that did not collect dust for the very good reason that the Midland kept its trains properly clean.

There was a feature of Midland carriage decoration which has been puzzling me of late. In Clayton's specifications for his original twelve-wheel composite coaches of 1875, he directed that the curtains (roller blinds had not yet appeared on the Midland) were to be stamped with the monogram M.R. *and fish*. What was this fish? At first thought it suggests some mystic symbol, like the fish carved on early Christian graves. Looking back over more than 70 years, and without further information, one may only conclude that the creature stamped on the curtains was the heraldic dolphin which was the sinister supporter of the Midland coat of arms. Mr. Clayton may not have been quite sure of its zoological status, indeed, on looking at it closely the present writer is himself not too sure, for although it started off as a dolphin it finished up with a spadelike tail, evidently in sympathy with the even more extraordinary animals which formed the dexter supporter and the crest of the arms.

Those coats of arms were great features of all the old railway companies. The North Western, grandly arrogant, appropriated Britannia ruling the waves, adding a gentlemanly lion and a viaduct with a North Western train on it to the background scenery. Many companies simply shovelled up the arms of the principal cities and towns they served, tied a garter round them, inscribing it with the title of the railway, and left it at that. The Caledonian helped itself to the Scottish royal arms, and nobody seemed to mind. The Great Central used for the crest of its arms a nice front elevation, *proper*, of one of Harry Pollitt's best express engines.

The Midland, though a relative newcomer to London, having reached St. Pancras thirty years after the opening of Euston, was still one of the old guard among the British railways. Like the North Western, it was formed by amalgamation, but two years before, in 1844, and included in its constituent lines the ancient Leicester and Swannington. The actual constituent companies were the North Midland, the Midland Counties and the Birmingham and Derby Junction. In 1903 it absorbed the Belfast and Northern Counties Railway in Ireland, and a Northern Counties Committee, which still survives under the L.M.S.R., was appointed to work it. In 1912 it took in the London, Tilbury and Southend Railway, which had begun its life in closer association with the Great Eastern. The latter, incidentally, used to run quite a number of trains into St. Pancras, which it considered its "West End" terminus. The Midland, owned jointly with the London and South Western, the Somerset and Dorset system (taken over in 1875); the Midland and Great Northern Joint dated as such from 1893; and there were others. These two, however, are specified here as the Midland made itself responsible for their locomotive power. In its final form it owned 1,520 miles of route.

Next door to the Midland at St. Pancras there was the Great Northern at King's Cross. The two systems were about as unlike as two railways can be without the crude difference of excellence on the one side and superlative badness on the other. The Great Northern was not a bad railway, though except on its best Scotch or Leeds expresses its carriages could not compare with those of the Midland. Its engines, both Patrick Stirling's and Ivatt's, were great, and very fine to look at, too, in their bright grass green with Indian red underframes. The atmosphere of King's Cross was so completely unlike that at St. Pancras that one almost expected to see placards up to the effect that there was no connection with the establishment next door. There was the reek of South Yorkshire coal, more pungent than that of Nottingham coal in St. Pancras over the way. This still prevails. It needs greater changes than mere railway amalgamations to wipe out the individuality of King's Cross and St. Pancras. The two great clocks eyeing one another from the top of each building usually disagreed, and that on King's Cross, which had been a showpiece at the Great Exhibition of 1851, was generally the more exemplary timepiece of the two.

Your first sight of a Great Northern train, with its undersized six-wheel carriages finished in varnished teak, and plain of interior to the point of severity, was a bit of a shock if you had just come off the Midland. A Great Northern engine, whether it were an Ivatt Atlantic or an old Stirling with a domeless boiler and a most shapely brass safety-valve casing, resembled nothing on the Midland. Then there were the suburban trains. Both companies ran through trains on to the Underground at King's Cross (Metropolitan), but while those of the Midland passed under their company's terminus and emerged at a decent distance down the road towards Kentish Town, those of the Great Northern came fuming up the drain right alongside King's Cross, disturbing the main station with the shouting of their exhausts.

As a very little boy, I remember my sister going off to visit Scotch relatives in Caithness. For quite a long time, for I had not yet been taken to Scotland, I imagined that magnificent Great Northern Atlantic rushing without pause through the night and eventually finishing up at Thurso. I never quite forgave the Great Northern for coming to an end, so far as its Scotch expresses were concerned, at Doncaster, and even the fact that the Great Northern engines worked through to York did not entirely atone.

The Great Northern Railway Scotch expresses, likewise the Leeds diners, were very magnificent trains. The teak carriages, when clean, looked as beautiful as the dirty suburban ones of the same railway did not. Perhaps it was asking for trouble to adopt such a carriage livery for a railway which possessed nine tunnels between King's Cross and Stevenage, not to mention the widened lines of the Metropolitan over which the suburban trains ran to Moorgate. But the Great Northern carriages had always been finished in this style, and the London and North Eastern, when the time came, took the livery over with the rest of the property. Most imposing, to youthful eyes, was the pre-1914 Flying Scotsman, made up of stately twelve-wheelers, entirely clerestoried and very ornate as to the dining-car interiors. Some of these had seats exactly like theatre-stalls, with florid cast-iron frames and oval backs of buttoned-in green plush. Separate headrests above them prevented collision between passengers' heads when they leant back after a hearty meal. The Great Northern Railway was the first in Britain to put on a regular diner, with the Pullman "hotel car" *Prince of Wales*, placed on the Leeds service in 1879.

The Great Northern gave the impression of being a much larger railway than it really was, when viewed from the London end. In owned route mileage with 1,033 miles of first track, it was 84¾ miles shorter than the Caledonian, and nine miles longer than the London and South Western. It was rather more than a third the extent of the Great Western, but more than three times that of the Great North of Scotland. Route mileages, however, are misleading things when one calculates a railway company's importance. The Great Northern was, for instance, nearly 100 miles short of the Great Southern and Western, but its total engine mileage was about three times that of the Irish company, its total number of passengers about seven times and its goods tonnage about five times. A murrain on statistics, anyway! The Great Northern's atmosphere of greatness was brought about by those magnificent trains leaving King's Cross for Scotland each evening, or coming in, one after another, in the grey morning mists. Here, clearly, there were comparisons to be made with the twice-as-large London and North Western and Midland systems.

High over the Great Northern by Maiden Lane, in by Dalston Junction and thence out again to Bow and Poplar, ran the North London Railway. Its system was short enough—fourteen miles of route—but its trains went far afield. They were very remarkable trains. In 1868 William Adams built 4–4–0 tank locomotives with inclined outside cylinders; a very pretty, rather exotic, Dutch-looking engine, with much bright copper and brass. He also designed a standard train of close-coupled four-wheel carriages, prominently distinguished by guards' vans with enormous birdcage lookouts, internally furnished with small gasometers for the lighting of the carriages by coal gas. Those were the trains with which the North London conducted its passenger business in 1874. Those also, with but few modifications, such as removal of the coal gas, sobering the appearance of the engines and providing them with cabs, were the North London trains of 1914. Twenty years after, some of those carriages, by kind permission of the L.M.S., were still bumping inflexibly up and down the Northern Heights.

Strangers either thought the North London trains deplorable, or else enjoyed in them a rare antique quality. At the age of four I made a terrible hullaballoo on being propelled into such a train at Gunnersbury. But two years later, I chose the journey from Willesden to Hammersmith via South Acton for a birthday treat. That was not strictly on the North London, but the North and South Western Junction Railway, over which the N.L.R. trains ran to Richmond. The Hammersmith branch, terminating at a narrow village platform tucked away behind the Chiswick High Road, was once worked by the only locomotive ever owned by the N. and S.W.J.R., a small saddle tank, but the North London purchased this and converted her into a breakdown crane engine. The Hammersmith and Chiswick passenger service, latterly worked by a London and North Western steam car, ceased in 1917, but the old crane engine, built in 1857, still survives on the L.M.S. at Bow.

The North London Railway brought you into Broad Street, that elevated chunk of Victorian-French-Baroque with the great sprawl of Liverpool Street under its grimy wing. But

Broad Street was also the City Terminus of the London and North Western, which ran a Birmingham business express service from it. The two companies had half-shares in Broad Street, which, however, was in style typical of the North London's shabby chateaux. So characteristic was the time-honoured North London suburban train—the black 4–4–0 tank engine, usually with inclined outside cylinders, the beetle-browed, window-barred four-wheel carriages and high-lan-terned, scarlet-ended vans, and the three-four rhythm of wheels on railjoints, that to a latter-day visitor who knew the old company there is still something improbable about the L.M.S. electric trains running in and out of Broad Street to-day.

Two Oxford men were in Ely one day. Earlier on they had been in Cambridge, and had satisfied themselves that, Backs or no Backs, it had nothing like the High. Now they stared at Ely station, at its two square wings with a colonnade and a sort of lantern between.

"Good Lord!" said one. "It's Queen's!"

The old Great Eastern station of Ely is still there, like many much older things, though something modernistic has happened to its outlines. Even so, for long the Great Eastern system was less changed by the amalgamations of 1923 than any other English railway. A Great Eastern express was neat and gaudy. The older engines were plain and severe of outline, as might have been expected, seeing that T. W. Worsdell and James Holden, who succeeded him at Stratford, were both of the Society of Friends. But theirs was a colour scheme so rich as to be something of an acquired taste to strangers, like the cookery of Tudor England.

Other railways had blue locomotives, but it took the Great Eastern to gild the iris. The blue Claud Hamiltons, the T19's, the mixed traffics and the little tanks were all additionally adorned with polished brass, vermilion side rods and lining-out, and had great castings of the Great Eastern's elaborately compound coat of arms in full colour adorning the driving wheel splashers.

Carriage decoration burgeoned on many lines more richly than harmoniously during the early nineteen-hundreds, but only the Great Eastern went so far as to trim its main-line third class with turkey-red velvet. In 1884, it was the first railway company to enliven the facias above the seat backs with mounted photographs of places on its system. Other companies imitated, but by the turn of the century the Great Eastern had got to the length of putting coloured transparencies of Cromer, Felixstowe and Southwold on the clerestory decklights. By contrast it had, where modern rolling stock was concerned, the grimmest, hardest, six-a-side third-class suburban carriages in the country. They were the North London brought up to date. But as hard words have been said about Great Eastern suburban trains over several generations, be it remembered that those bleak and severe thirds were designed for workmen coming begrimed from their labours, that a second class was retained for season-ticket holders, that the company encouraged the cheap traveller on a scale unparalleled, and that it operated in and out of Liverpool Street, supplemented by Fenchurch Street, a steam suburban service second to none in smartness and frequency.

There was pride and quality in its best expresses; the Norfolk Coast Express, with its non-stop run to North Walsham; the Hook-of-Holland Express, most sumptuous of Continentals, whereon you could get one of the best, and certainly the most smartly served restaurant-car dinners in the world, and that other Continental express running from Harwich to the North *via* Ely and March, providing an object lesson in cross-country working. The Great Eastern Railway had 1,258½ miles of route, including joint lines.

Fenchurch Street also served as terminus the London, Tilbury and Southend Railway, a system which the Great Eastern worked until its lease finished in 1875. In 1880 William Adams, who had been with the Great Eastern until 1878 and had then gone to the London and South Western, anonymously designed for the Tilbury a magnificent 4–4–2 express tank engine, a basic design which lasted so long that T. Whitelegg's final, much enlarged version continued to be built after the L.M.S. had taken over. For locomotives with 6 ft. 6 in. coupled wheels, the larger Tilbury engines had remarkable powers of acceleration; they would walk off with a thirteen-coach business train with almost the smartness of a Great Eastern suburban tank and then work it up to a gait more like that of the magnificent *Abergavenny* and *Bessborough* on the Brighton expresses. An interesting feature of this company was the through service which it operated from Southend to Ealing *via* the District Railway.

The Tilbury was one of those companies that named their engines impartially after places along the line. You saw *Southend-on-Sea* perversely running towards London, and Mr. Whitelegg clearly saw nothing funny in having an engine named *Burdett Road*. At the end of last century, the Midland built a connecting link from South Tottenham, and in 1912, the Tilbury was amalgamated into the Midland. Tilbury green vanished under Midland red, which also covered those names which had once led so many old parties into the wrong train.

Not many recall the steam Underground with affection, though its brimstonian deeps are supposed to have cured several bad asthma cases and there are also couples living who, in the days before dark cinemas were invented, cuddled in the gassy gloom of a Metropolitan carriage rumbling round the Inner Circle in the off-peak hours. Still, some loved it for itself.

The standard Underground 4–4–0 condensing tank engine was so much a part of the system—both the Metropolitan and the District employed it—that other companies working through to the Underground in steam days (the Midland to Moorgate and the North Western on the Outer Circle from Broad Street to Mansion House) adopted the same design for these services. This may have been to save them the trouble of providing, as did the Great Northern, the London, Chatham and Dover, and the Great Western, condensing engines of their own design, but it looked as if they expected nothing else to "go" in the tunnels. The condensing gear, introduced by Daniel Gooch when the Metropolitan was first opened in 1863 and was worked for a while by the Great Western, was supposed to mitigate the foulness of the tunnels by absorbing the exhaust, but it did not eliminate the smoke nuisance.

There was something Miltonian about the steam Underground, especially on the section underneath the Euston Road during the evening rush. Gower Street* to Baker Street was a terror. On the District there was the more occasional thrill of running awash beneath Hammersmith Broadway, where the station and the tunnel had a bad habit of flooding.

The first electric tubes were received with delight, and in their early days had plenty of individuality—the City and South London with its peculiar smell, its gin-bottle locomotives and padded-cell cars; the Central London with its quite lordly-looking coaches and, for a few years, really imposing double- bogie electric engines. Interest wilted with the coming of the prosaic motor coach; the best thing about the Bakerloo was its name.

Crossing London River; the railway system of Kent was one of the most individual, most important, best of a kind, worst of a kind, most delightful and most detestable in Great Britain. The South Eastern Railway and the London, Chatham and Dover Railway had each a few good trains and some decent rolling stock. James Stirling's locomotives on the South Eastern, plain, domeless and dour, were none the less excellent, indeed, much too good for the majority of the trains they had to run. The Wainwrights' main-line carriages were admirable; the first class were as good as any in the country, and where, on the northern lines, second class remained static until it was simply third class with a mat added, the South Eastern seconds attained Continental standards.

But with about a siding-full of shining exceptions, the thirds were shocking things, ancient, pokey and fly-blown. Some choice specimens are illustrated. They were quite good by the standards of the early 'sixties. In the 'eighties such things, close-coupled into suburban rakes, were still conveying the respectable white-collar man between his place of employ and his home on the Mid-Kent line. By the 'nineties they had come down in the world, but were travelling farther afield, taking the fruit-picker to Paddock Wood, the hopper to Headcorn, the Sunday school to Hastings, and Bill and his girl to Folkestone

* Now Euston Square.

for the day. By then the tyres had collected so many flats that each wheel was an irregular polygon, and the motion at various speeds was interesting.

The South Eastern and the Chatham led a violently quarrelsome existence in their long-suffering county. The Chatham was the incomer, not having begun business until 1858, and then only as the bucolic East Kent Railway between Strood and Faversham. It assumed its more imposing title in the following year, having progressed westwards to St. Mary Cray. By various dodgings and running powers it had reached Victoria in 1861. Going east, it reached Dover in the same year. It finally got a good hold on the Thanet resorts, and a new Continental route to Flushing *via* Queenborough.

As well as providing a main line in opposition to the South Eastern, it irritated the latter by sly pinpricks at Sevenoaks, Ashford, Gravesend and other places. While the South Eastern endeavoured to do business on the lines of forcing passengers into the second class by making the third pre-eminently awful— a policy openly proclaimed by the chairman, Sir Edward Watkin—the Chatham owed many of its shortcomings to pure and simple poverty. It was in Queer Street in its early days.

But it possessed a bonny fighter in its chairman, James Staats Forbes. South Eastern, and Chatham, fought their bitter feud among the hop-gardens and oast houses, and built or worked a considerable number of important London stations against each other. Everybody, therefore, was surprised when, at the beginning of 1899, instead of their chairmen meeting in final bloody combat in a secluded glade of Chislehurst Common, there was suddenly a South Eastern and Chatham Railway, worked by a Managing Committee of the two companies.

The London, Chatham and Dover, as the London Smash'em and Turnover, was the only British railway to have a rhyming slang nickname. It also went in for unconventional names for many of its locomotives, during the early and middle years. There were five Crampton's patent engines skittishly entitled *Flirt, Coquette, Sylph, Echo* and *Flora*. There were two consecutive locomotives named *Huz* and *Buz*. During one insolvent phase of the company's history the locomotive superintendent, then Mr. Martley, remarked that owing to continual laying-off of the Longhedge Works staff, it was an enigma to him that his latest express engine had ever been finished. And *Enigma* she became, officially entitled on two handsome brass plates.

The South Eastern had that surprising branch to Reading. Down through the Surrey heaths and below the chalk by Dorking and Betchworth came strange, foreign trains—old Cudworth 2–4–0 locomotives hauling Great Western clerestory carriages—providing through services between North-West and South-East. Later, the South Eastern and Chatham built some quite pretentious tricomposite corridor brake carriages for the through trains. These, admirable vehicles for their time, designed by Harry Wainwright, have had a long—perhaps too long—but honourable career. In 1943 I was unsuccessfully shot up in one by a Focke-Wulf 190 between Dunton Green and Polhill Tunnel.

As the South Eastern and Chatham, the united Kentish companies led, apart from an imposing Continental service, a shabby-genteel existence for the rest of their history. Harry Wainwright succeeded Stirling of the South Eastern and William Kirtley of the Chatham as locomotive superintendent. His locomotives, for the most part, were things of gorgeous beauty with brass domes and chimney caps. The other day I saw one of them at Charing Cross; the paint had peeled off her brazen dome casing and some industrious party had rubbed it up bright.

"I remember," I began, "when I was a boy——"

"Yes," said the driver sombrely. "I remember when I was a boy, too. I had to clean the flicking things!"

In the thirty odd years from 1874, the London, Brighton and South Coast Railway was a system that struck you in the eye. It served a happy part of England. Brighton, Boxhill, Ashdown Forest, the glorious downland from Beachy Head to Singleton— all belonged to it. Its locomotives were magnificent. A Stroudley locomotive was the work of an artist for—supreme test—it looked beautiful even in the working drawings.

An artist's work, too, was in the colour scheme of a Brighton train under William Stroudley and his successor, the elder Billinton, who copied him in this feature. It was, with that of the Great Eastern, one of the most elaborate liveries in railway history. But Holden of the Great Eastern was a Philistine. He gave us the colours of a showman, not of an artist. This is a cold, considered opinion of maturity; as a child I thought the Great Eastern superb and the Brighton yellow engines exotic but ugly, not to be appreciated until, years after, I saw Stroudley's *Gladstone* at York Museum and Dr. Bradbury Winter's lovely model of *Como* in the Brighton Art Gallery. There was only one carriage livery that could harmonize with "Stroudley's Improved Engine Green" and that was the rich mahogany, used on the Brighton from the 'forties until 1903.

Like the Chatham and the Great Eastern, the London, Brighton and South Coast had seen evil days, at one stage having its engines seized for debt. It was encircled by enemies and it fought them with spirit. It had won a pitched battle with the London and South Western at Havant in 1858, with cudgels, blocked crossings and lifted rails. Latterly it went in for building strategic lines against the South Eastern. Those lovely winding routes through East Sussex south of Eridge were directed at keeping the South Eastern out of Eastbourne, indeed, this sort of thing was a leading cause of Brighton impoverishment. The old spirit died hard; in 1919 a South Western porter at Midhurst "didn't know" the way to the Brighton station down the road, and his opposite number on the Brighton, learning that we had come in by the South Western from Petersfield, prevaricated about the time of the next train to Petworth.

The Brighton expresses were on the whole excellent. Those to Portsmouth were in competition with the South Western and passengers benefited accordingly. There were gorgeous Victorian Pullman cars with such names as *Pavilion* and *Albert Victor*, and elegant Edwardian ones such as *Grosvenor* and *Princess Helen*. There was the new Victoria Station (quite unconnected with the Chatham next door), with its enormously long platforms.

Likewise there was the hour-and-forty-minutes dawdle from Victoria to Dorking (27¾ miles *via* Selhurst), riding in the late Mr. Stroudley's poorest four-wheel third-class carriages behind Mr. Billinton's most sluggish tank engines, with a dreary change at Sutton thrown in by way of instructive exercise. The Brighton was a smart railway in some ways—the Southern Belle became a household word, and Soames Forsyte travelled in bleak luxury by the City Limited—while it gave wicked service in others. Apart from its Pullman cars, which it did not build, it had exactly three main-line corridor carriages, all in the special City Limited set of 1907.

Many of the old companies used to decorate engines on special occasions, and in the South of England particularly, great heights of gaudy magnificence were attained with the royal train engines. But the Brighton men were the masters of this pleasantly garish custom. Not only royalties and visiting French Presidents were thus honoured; terrific effects were achieved by New Cross and Battersea sheds in dressing engines for the annual staff outings. Brilliant flags and festoons, garlands and painted shields draped the gay yellow engines. Flight followed fancy until, in 1898, the proprietors of a widely popular weekly offered a prize for the best-dressed engine. Battersea went to the brilliant expedient of buying two half-life size Mediterranean figurines from a travelling showman and mounting them proudly on the front platform of Stroudley's *Allen Sarle*. It was masterly. The plaster nymph and shepherd came away to Eastbourne on the front of their engine at fifty glorious miles an hour. The prize went to Battersea and New Cross was left nowhere.

A picture of the London and South Western has already been given. Until the 'nineties, its local trains exemplified the same mean antiquity as its neighbours', but at the turn of the century there was a sweeping reform in this respect. As remarked, the company was at various times on terms of armed neutrality or in a state of open war with the London, Brighton and South Coast. Soon after the formation of the Southern Railway in 1923, a South Western guard told me that "that

45

line" (the Brighton) "belongs to us now." The South Western was, however, good neighbourly with the South Eastern at Guildford and Reading, for the Brighton was their common enemy. At the same time, it was most distant with the South Eastern's Great Western friends, who had a proprietorial attitude towards Exeter and Plymouth. The South Western's most masterly piece of strategy was the purchase, at a remote date in history, of the Bodmin and Wadebridge Railway in Cornwall. Thereafter, in the course of long years, it gradually extended its own main system to meet the captured outpost, thus effectively keeping the Great Western off the Atlantic Coast between Minehead and Newquay.

The Great Western, even the smaller, pre-grouping Great Western, was the giant of British railways. It had always been a giant, even when it was simply an unbranching, rigid and baulky road from Paddington Green to a timber barn containing four tracks and a sector-table at Bristol. Its original, tragic, heroic broad gauge of 7 ft. 0¼ in. (gorgeous dimension, impossible anywhere but in England!) gave all its equipment a giant quality from the first. As the years passed, it absorbed its old allies and some of its old enemies. The Bristol and Exeter, the South Devon, the Cornwall, the West Cornwall, the South Wales, the West Midland—which last, in the great days of its piratical independence had, in alliance with the North Western, fought the Great Western with a Euston to Worcester and Wolverhampton service *via* Bletchley and Yarnton—all came in the end to swell the Great Western system, just as most of the independent Welsh railways did anew in 1923. In 1914, the Great Western had 3,028 miles of route.

But come back to the Paddington of the middle 'seventies, and the Great Western Railway as it was about the beginning of our period! The station is the Paddington that Frith painted. It is the same changeless Paddington that we see to-day. But take a look at the Flying Dutchman about to leave for the West! The eight-wheel carriages, apart from their immortal chocolate and cream livery, and one other thing, resemble Clayton's new and stately clerestory vehicles on the Midland. But in these of

46

the Great Western, full advantage has been taken of the broad gauge, for they have bodies 10 ft. 6 in. wide. How different a thing the corridor train might have been if—but the broad gauge has been dead for more than half a century now! The broad gauge was dying even then, in the 'seventies. New rolling stock was being made convertible—even those magnificent carriages were designed to have their internal partitions cropped and the sides pushed in.

But the most extraordinary thing about the long-impending abolition of the broad gauge concerned the express locomotives. Daniel Gooch designed a standard broad-gauge express engine in the middle 'forties—*Great Western*, which was experimental, in 1846, and *Iron Duke*, the class prototype, a year later. With slight modifications, including increased boiler power, the *Iron Duke* class remained the standard broad-gauge express engine until the end of the 'eighties, and it is inevitably a Gooch eight-foot single, with its sandwich frames, domeless boiler and tall copper-capped chimney that heads the *Flying Dutchman* in our retrospective view of Paddington. Only right at the end of the broad-gauge period were more advanced passenger locomotives built for the West of England trains (most of the rest of the system was converted to standard gauge at variously earlier dates), and these, designed by William Dean, were made easily convertible, with the wheels temporarily outside both sets of double frames.

Then, and through most phases of its history, the Great Western was, and has been, an extraordinary mixture of the modern and the ancient, the smart and the dilatory, the enterprising and the lethargic. It has held world speed records, both a century ago and in our own time. With the opening of the Ashendon-Aynho line in 1910 it began a two-hour service to Birmingham in opposition to the North Western; later we shall recall its test matches with the South Western in competition for the American services from Plymouth; before 1914 it ran to Bristol, $117\frac{1}{2}$ miles, in 2 hours; to Plymouth, $225\frac{3}{4}$ miles, in 4 hours 7 minutes, without a stop; to Cardiff, $145\frac{1}{4}$ miles, in 2 hours 50 minutes. At the same time its local trains meandered from station to station and seemed, as indeed they still do, to sit down for five minutes and take in water at every other station at least. No trains have ever beaten Great Western locals for the number of times it is deemed necessary for them to take water. The Great Western has been the first to do a remarkable number of things. It had the first eight-wheel main-line carriages in the country—the Long Charleys of 1852—it built the prototype of the modern sleeping car in 1881, that of the standard British corridor train in 1891; brilliant critical expositions have failed to destroy its reputation for having been the first British railway to run a train at over 100 miles an hour; G. J. Churchward built for it in the early years of this century locomotives which were some fifteen years ahead of those on other systems.

But to earlier generations, Great Western meant broad gauge, and broad gauge, Great Western. Monumental nuisance though it was, in spite of the laying of extra rails forming mixed gauge, those who knew it swore by it. It lingered on the main line to the West after it had vanished utterly from the Midlands and from South Wales. But the end came at last, in 1892. By then the only unmixed broad gauge left on the Great Western was between Exeter and Penzance, with branches. Some of it was on cross-sleepered road with bullhead rails, but most was the old baulk road with bridge rails on longitudinal sleepers, capable of narrowing by cutting the transverse transoms and pushing in the offside timbers and rails.

On May 20th, every broad-gauge locomotive and vehicle west of Exeter was worked eastwards to Swindon for scrapping or conversion. The last broad-gauge Cornishman, hauled by the *Great Western*, left Paddington, in the presence of a huge crowd, at 10.15 a.m., running through to Penzance. It returned, stopping at all stations, through the night to Swindon, being the last broad-gauge train of any kind to travel over the line from Penzance to Exeter. In its wake, the three-days' job of conversion immediately began. When it finally rolled into Swindon at 4.0 a.m. on the 21st, the broad gauge was dead in that West Country where it had held out for so long.* Its ghost haunted

---

* The last broad-gauge train *into* London was the up night mail, arriving at Paddington on the morning of May 21st; engine, *Bulkeley*.

Cambridge in 1900: Left is Great Northern Railway 0–4–2 No. 112 (Patrick Stirling) on a Hitchin train; on the right is a Great Eastern express from Hunstantor to Liverpool Street, headed by J. Holden's class T 19 seven-footer No. 735

Swindon for near a couple of years after, in the shape of two
4–4–0 saddle-tank engines, *Stag* and *Leopard*, whose last duties
were to shunt condemned locomotives and vehicles in the miles
of scrap sidings that had been laid down.

The broad gauge did not vanish unsung. *Punch* published a
cartoon of a locomotive being interred and a parody on *The
Burial of Sir John Moore*. An anonymous writer produced something that reached greater heights. It began:—

> Gone is the Broad Gauge of our youth,
> Its splendid course is run.
> It has fought the battle nobly,
> But the Narrow Gauge has won.
> Alas for good Sir Daniel!
> Alas for bold Brunel!
> They are resting from their labours;
> They are sleeping: it is well!

And the last verse ran:—

> Resistless ran *Tornado*,
> And *Amazon* could breast
> The fury of the tempest
> In her journeys to the West.
> *Lord of the Isles, Great Britain,*
> These, and a hundred more
> That sped along the railway
> In the good old days of yore—
> We have lost them! We have lost them!
> But we loved them in their prime,
> And their names shall long re-echo
> Down the corridors of time!

# CHAPTER III

## THE OLD COMPANIES

### —Continued

THERE was no Great Central Railway in 1874. But there was the Manchester, Sheffield and Lincolnshire Railway. It was a northern line; its home was on the bare Pennines, in the reeking valleys below them, and on the windy East Coast, and when at last, having become the Great Central in 1897, it reached Marylebone in the spring of 1899, it was still hard for some to regard it as one of London's railways. Marylebone was rather the terminus of the Sheffield company's London branch line, and it preserved something of that atmosphere; Mgr. Ronald Knox once remarked that no London station was more full of bird song. To this day it is only too obvious that the passenger station was intended to be twice as big as it is. The London extension was viewed with pessimism at the time of its inception; if M.S. and L. had stood for "Money Sunk and Lost," G.C. clearly meant "Gone Completely."

But if, in very truth, that London extension was but a branch line, it was certainly a very fine branch. The first Great Central London expresses showed a higher proportion of corridor stock than those of any other railway; they were lightly loaded and smartly timed; internally they were most comfortable while they perpetuated the old Sheffield company's partiality for gorgeous decoration; Jason sought for the Golden Fleece in mezzotint panels on the dining-car ceilings, and as you lounged on a splendiferous pew of carved oak and figured plush, the sun, shining through coloured glass decklights, gave a deliciously bizarre quality to the complexion of the lady opposite. There were buffet cars, long before any other company dared to introduce such things. While the Pullman Car Company claimed to operate such vehicles, the Pullman "buffet" was simply a pantry at that time, and had nothing so convenient and companionable as a bar.

Then there were the Great Central London suburban trains, which were superior to those of the Great Western and the Metropolitan, with which they had to share most of their traffic. The later Great Central suburban stock, high, wide, and handsome, with reading lamps just where they were wanted on the facias behind the seats, was easily the best in Great Britain, and the 4–6–2 suburban tank engines introduced by J. G. Robinson at the end of our period were in sharp contrast to the swarms of small and fussy antiques which served other London dormitories.

But at the other end of the system, the atmosphere was still Manchester, Sheffield and Lincolnshire rather than Great Central. A suburban train serving all stations from Manchester London Road to Glossop was a very different thing from that between Marylebone and Aylesbury. There was the same difference between a Manchester-Cleethorpes express and a Manchester-London express. The London extension was the Great Central's show piece, and its trains, in competition with the much older-established trains of the North Western, the Midland and the Great Northern, were gradely things indeed. Viewed dispassionately, one of Robinson's Great Central Atlantic engines was a most shapely machine. Those who knew them not admired, and those who did know them swore that no other engines could touch them for appearance. In the early years of this century, they worked the fastest train out of London, running non-stop from Marylebone to Sheffield in 170 minutes for the 164¾ miles. Fast running was nothing new to this company; on November 6, 1888, the old Parker 2–4–0 engine No. 79 ran a special of five twelve-wheel carriages from Manchester to Aintree, on the Cheshire Lines, in 34 minutes for the 35 miles, including the severe slack between Halewood and Gateacre. The Cheshire Lines, with its Liverpool and Manchester expresses in competition with the North Western, was a favourite sprinting ground for the Sheffield or Great Central engines which worked most of its trains. As a joint railway, it survived grouping; much of its system is in Lancashire.

The Great Central London extension might have been described as part of a North Country plot to capture Continental Europe. The Imperial Watkin of the South Eastern was equally imperial in respect of the M.S. and L. and the Metropolitan Railways, and his machinations were behind the Channel Tunnel Company as well. But the Manchester, Sheffield and Lincolnshire Railway never succeeded in running a train into the Gare du Nord. The nearest it got was to build a royal saloon in 1883 for the South Eastern, which kept it at Calais for royal trips abroad. An attempt was made to assassinate Edward VII in it at Brussels. A late addition to the Great Central game-bag was the Lancashire, Derbyshire and East Coast Railway, which had ambitious schemes on the lines suggested by its title, with a spectacular passage of the Peak District. But the L.D. and E.C. never grew beyond a headless and tailless trunk, connecting the Dukeries with Lincoln, but failing to serve Lancashire or Derbyshire and never reaching the East Coast. During its short active career from 1896 to December 31, 1906, it was worked by a handful of black 0–4–4, 0–6–2 and 0–6–4 tank engines, and its passenger needs were served by red six-wheel carriages of commonplace type. The Great Central had 628 miles of route in 1914.

Rather more fortunate than the L.D. and E.C. was the Hull and Barnsley Railway, which began in a very independent way at Cannon Street Station, Hull, and ended, according to a classic description, in a field near Cudworth. Its bread and butter came from the West Riding and from extensive docks on the Humber. From 1880, when it was incorporated, until 1905, when it assumed officially its commonly used name, its correct title was Hull, Barnsley and West Riding Junction Railway and Dock Company. Travellers knew it, however, by a quite creditable express service which it ran between Hull and Sheffield, worked by locomotives with the characteristic domeless boiler and round-topped cab of the Stirling family.

A Lancashire and Yorkshire train was a dour thing if you were not used to it. No brilliant colour schemes here; no names to the engines to gentle the condition of their severe black colour and puritanical outlines. The carriages had a two-colour finish, but the two colours were much of a muchness, brown above and dark brown below. Nor did their exteriors belie their interiors: there was an overstuffed pomposity about the first class, and in the thirds there was slippery horsehair below and white matchboarding above in all but the best stock.

Back in the 'seventies, the Lanky was a fearsome railway, ancient in equipment, dreary in its stations, one of which had once had the Brontë sisters' scapegrace brother for a booking-clerk, hopelessly inadequate and congested in its important station layouts. Then something happened to it. Barton Wright began, and Sir John Aspinall completed a revolution in its standard of locomotive power; the services were smartened up in speed and frequency, it was a pioneer in electrification, and in many ways became a model undertaking for the needs of the country it served. The austere appearance of its trains was perhaps natural: reformed rakes usually run to asceticism. There was reason for those shiny horsehair seats, too; they were proof against the grease of the factory and the fluff of the cotton-mill which decorated the persons of thousands of the company's regular clients. The L. and Y.R. owned 600 miles of route.

There was a sombre grandeur about the fast, short-distance expresses serving the Lancashire valleys, hauled by energetic superheater 2–4–2 tank engines; in the ungainly symmetry of Aspinall's inside-cylinder ("Highflyer") Atlantics, somehow suggesting feminine costume of the year of their appearance, 1899; in the business expresses that roared over the Pennines from Manchester to Leeds, all suggesting scenery for a Priestley story. One of the *Good Companions* came a cropper on a North Eastern platform, but most of their journeys sounded as if they were on the Lancashire and Yorkshire.

From 1879 to 1897, when the Lanky absorbed it, there was a small but plucky little railway suggesting the sturdy local independence of early days, and that was the West Lancashire. It connected Preston and Blackburn with the superior resort of Southport, while the L. and Y. performed a similar office for the more proletarian and more remunerative Blackpool. The West Lancashire, considering its smallness, had a remarkable locomotive stock. Its most modern passenger engines, built new, were 0–4–2's of sober and formal aspect, but at second-hand, from the London, Brighton and South Coast, it acquired some most picturesque old stagers; there were Craven 2–2–2's, which had once gone spinning down to Portsmouth, and 2–4–0's which had plodded across the Weald with Brighton excursions of caravan length; there was a truly choice old Brighton 0–6–0 goods with a Wilson fluted dome. Of tank engines, there were three extraordinary little 0–4–0's with outside frames and cranks. One of these survives at the time of writing on the Liverpool Overhead Railway, which uses it for shunting, for ballasting at night when the current is off, and for clearing ice from conductor rails. The W.L.R. locomotive stock was of harlequin appearance; when first acquired, the Brighton express engines were still in Stroudley's yellow, while the 0–4–2's were purple. The only other purple engine I know of in Britain was Beattie's *Herod* (delicious name!) on the London and South Western, which was thus painted for some time in the 'sixties.

Judged by even the main-line standards of its day, the West Lancashire had excellent carriages. Of rather Great Western aspect with clerestory roofs, they were steam heated, and that some twenty years before most companies discarded the ancient tin footwarmer. Steam was supplied, not by the locomotives, but by boilers in the vans, the protruding chimneys of which greatly mystified uninformed passers-by at Preston.

Judgment by incidental reference in the works of Arnold Bennett and H. G. Wells would not suggest any unusual excellence about the North Staffordshire Railway, yet this was another local system with numerous good points. Latterly it was one of those railways which used only electric light in its carriages. Even the lordly Midland, ten years after the smash and the fire at Ais Gill, had plenty of gas left on its trains, indeed, to this day, the Southern is the only British main-line railway to have got rid of it completely. The North Stafford had its home in the reeking trough of the Five Towns, a close-knit, contorted system. There were loop lines in various parts of England, but the Loop Line meant that of only one railway, the North Stafford. The company made use of extensive running powers, being on good terms with its various neighbours. The distinctive red North Stafford trains ran north to Manchester, London Road, over the North Western, east to Derby and Nottingham over the Midland and the Great Northern, and southwards, on the London and North Western again, to Wolverhampton, Birmingham and Rugby. Jointly with the North Western, it operated the through express service from Manchester to London *via* Stoke.

As unlike the Loop Line as any railway could be was the Leek and Manifold Valley, eight miles of 2 ft. 3 in. gauge; a gorgeous line in a gorgeous country, perhaps comparable with the Vale of Rheidol and the Lynton and Barnstaple. Yet this was worked by the North Stafford, and from its opening in 1904 to the time when the L.M.S. (which eventually closed it down) took over, its squat, busy tank engines with their enormous headlamps, and its sightseeing saloon carriages were painted in the crimson of Stoke.

Down in the South Midlands, stretching from the Midland and the North Western systems, westwards below the green ridge of Edge Hill to Stratford-on-Avon and Broom, was the Stratford-on-Avon and Midland Junction Railway, a cross-country line having but 67½ miles of route, including the branches to Blisworth and Cockley Brake Junction (for Banbury). The company came into being at the end of our period, having been formed in 1908 by amalgamation of the East and West Junction Railway (Towcester to Stratford), the Evesham, Redditch and Stratford-on-Avon Junction (Stratford Junction to Broom), and the Stratford-on-Avon, Towcester and Midland Junction Railway, which provided the natural eastern outlet to the Midland Railway. The S.M.J. was noteworthy, in the latter part of its short life as a united system, in having no tank locomotives. When the old "express" engines of the E. and W.J. had vanished—they were Beyer Peacock 2–4–0 tanks—the only strictly passenger type the company possessed was a solitary 2–4–0 tender engine, also by Beyer Peacock, but much more modern than the tanks. The rest of the locomotive stock consisted of 0–6–0 goods engines, twelve Beyer Peacocks with double frames, supplemented, after our period, by another solitary, namely, a Stroudley goods bought at second-hand from the London, Brighton and South Coast. The S.M.J. proudly styled itself the Shakespeare Route, but it had its roots in iron ore rather than tourists. It was a jolly little line while it lasted.

Before going north again, we may notice the two joint railways owning their own locomotives and rolling stock, the Midland and Great Northern and the Somerset and Dorset. They need no geographical particulars here, for they are still with us though no longer owning their own motive power. But they had their independent days. The largest component of the M.G.N. was the Eastern and Midlands, comprising that part of the line lying east of Lynn. It was also the last to be included in the joint undertaking, a proud rural main line with handsome 4–4–0 express engines savouring, like many of Beyer Peacock's, of the practice of William Adams. Through the long years of joint operation these old stagers survived, alongside standard Midland and Great Northern types of Johnson and Ivatt design respectively, and painted a glorious golden ochre. The M. and G.N. was surely the only railway to possess an Elizabethan station—not the mock Tudor edifices that rambled and blossomed from the Wall to the Channel, but the genuine article. Bourne Station was previously the Old Red House, once the country residence of Sir Everard Digby, the Gunpowder Plot conspirator.

Before the Midland and the South Western took it over jointly, in 1876, the Somerset and Dorset was a much less respectable concern than the Eastern and Midlands became in its last years. Its engines were small and ancient, of its carriages the less said the better, and its services were crawling and casual. The most exciting thing a Somerset and Dorset train ever did was the extraordinary antic by which, long ago, it gained access to the London and South Western junction at Templecombe. This operation still entails backing in or backing out, for northbound and southbound trains respectively, but in the old days, with a spur line to the South Western in the Salisbury direction, there was a double movement, in the course of which the train crossed over its own path at right angles.

Almost the first thing the Somerset and Dorset did after the Joint Committee took over was to stage a head-on collision of spectacular dimensions, under the most discreditable circumstances (Radstock, August 27, 1876), but joint operation by two such highly respectable partners as the South Western and the Midland had a lasting salutary effect. The Midland became responsible for the locomotives, though the carriages were of individual design. They were quite remarkably good carriages, combining noticeable features of those belonging to both owning companies. A Somerset and Dorset train, royal blue from end to end, was an extremely handsome spectacle.

But it was up in the far north-west of England that you found trains which were truly red-white-and-blue. There was art in them, though; this was no mere tricolour abomination. The Furness locomotives were a rich Indian red—a shade, I believe, introduced to the district by Tulk and Ley of Whitehaven, builders of the famous Crampton engines for the North Western, Liège and Namur, South Eastern and other railways a century ago. The carriages, at one time red like the engines, were blue in their latter days, with white upper panels. A Furness train looked at its best in strong evening sunshine between showers, with the rainy Cumbrian hills all around.

Right up to the end of last century, the Furness Railway retained a number of very archaic locomotives on light goods work, these being 0–4–0 tender engines of Edward Bury's classic design with bar frames and haycock fireboxes. The most famous, old *Coppernob*, now a hundred years old, was one of the company's original engines. In retirement she was housed in a sort of glass pagoda at Barrow Central Station. One night during the war, the Germans gave Barrow a bad time, and among other things bombed the station, blowing *Coppernob's* glass house to pieces. But the old engine stood up bravely among the ruins. Quite a number of people felt happier amongst the wreckage for seeing her thus, ancient yet invincible.

Another Furness goods, at a much earlier date, had a less lucky adventure. This was No. 115, a Sharp Stewart 0–6–0 built in 1881. At Lindal, on September 22, 1892, there was a sudden colliery subsidence, forming a funnel-shaped hole into which No. 115 took a header. The tender was saved, but the engine sank rapidly through loose earth and coal waste to a great depth, becoming a total loss. There she remains to-day, far down below the present L.M.S. tracks on Lindal Bank, unseen of men for more than half a century.

About the turn of the century, the Furness had an inspiration, that of replacing second class by a reserved-third class, whereby, by paying more, third-class passengers could be sure of a seat, and that in a carriage which would carry no casual ordinary travellers. The passenger who had paid for his privilege was thus protected against the discomfort of crowded accommodation. Unfortunately the company got into trouble over the legality of such a proceeding, and the thing had to be dropped. Furness carriages were modern and conveniently arranged. It seemed, however, that the third-class seats had been designed for persons of enormous development as to the back, but with thighs so short as to need a perch rather than a seat. Not even the slippery horsehair of the Lanky could beat the Furness seats in the gentle art of sliding the drowsy passenger neatly on to the floor.

Cumbria is a small country, the severed end of that little kingdom of Strathclyde, once stretching from Lancaster to Dumbarton Rock, but a country it has always been; no mere province. A Cumbrian mountain is a little thing, but it is every inch a mountain, unlike many far bigger eminences. And in the days of the old railway companies, the Furness was not the only railway Cumbria possessed. There was, and owing to joint interests, there still is the Cockermouth, Keswick and Penrith, a vassal of both the London and North Western and the North-Eastern, which worked its traffic. On it you could enjoy the experience of a superb ride along the length of Bassenthwaite Lake, with Skiddaw rising beyond the water and *Skiddaw*, a North Western Jumbo, fussing along at the head of the train. This sort of experience, common on the Highland Railway, was rare in England.

Farther north lay the Maryport and Carlisle. It was only $42\frac{3}{4}$ miles long—12 miles longer than the Cockermouth—but unlike the latter it had always worked its own traffic with, save for a quaint exception, its own rolling stock. That exception belonged to the latter days of its existence. It was a single London and North Western corridor coach, scrupulously lettered: *On loan to the Maryport and Carlisle Railway*, and it formed the daily through train from Keswick (C.K. and P.R.) to Carlisle, *via* Cockermouth, Bullgill and Wigton. Small though it was, the Maryport and Carlisle was a patriarch among British railways, its oldest section was opened in July, 1840. During our period its trains had a Scottish, rather than an English aspect, the locomotives of Campbell and Smellie having decided affinities to the Stirling school. Hugh Smellie, indeed, succeeded James Stirling on the Glasgow and South Western.

A former Bishop of Ripon once excused himself for lateness at a meeting in Knaresborough by mentioning casually that there was such a thing as the North Eastern Railway, and a juror got away with the same excuse. That was the old, easy-going North Eastern of the 'seventies; the line that had the fatherly Edward Fletcher in charge of its locomotive department and its engines adorned according to the fancy of the drivers. The easy going was often past a joke, not only in punctuality, as just suggested; examination of boilers was not a strong point, and quite a surprising number of Fletcher's engines blew up at various times.

The North Eastern was pre-eminently a child of amalgamations. It was formed in 1854 out of the Leeds Northern, York and North Midland, and York, Newcastle and Berwick Railways. The last-mentioned in turn was a fusion of the Great North of England, Newcastle and Darlington Junction, alias York and Newcastle, and Newcastle and Berwick Railways, with others thrown in. In 1863 the company took in the Stockton and Darlington, opened in 1825 as the first public steam railway in the world. Counting all its minor constituents, the North Eastern in its final form, with 1,754 miles of route, consisted of about fifty once independent railways. In the old days, many of these mixed origins remained apparent in its trains. The individuality of the Stockton and Darlington survived amalgamation for a long time; William Bouch went on designing locomotives at Darlington while Fletcher built other, quite different engines at Gateshead. There were variations in livery between Gateshead, Darlington and Leeds, at which last Leeds Northern traditions lingered.

Not until the 'eighties did the North Eastern become more or less homogenous. Thereafter it grew into a very great, very powerful and very respectable railway, with ambitious tendencies. At intervals there was evidence of designs on the Great Northern with a view to putting London on the North Eastern map; sumptuous offices in neo-Queen Anne style were built and opened in Cowley Street, Westminster. It has even been said that the North Eastern's plans really took shape, and that the London and North Eastern of 1923 was simply the North Eastern aggrandized into an imperial power. It is certainly amusing, if no more, to observe the facile way in which the initials L.N.E.R. become abbreviated into N.E. on one pretext or another. Yet, in its great days, the North Eastern retained a few features that were surprisingly archaic. It stuck to slotted-post signals to the last, and although, after the Midland, it had the most comfortable ordinary trains in the country, most of these were lighted by gas.

It was an imposing line, straight and level across the Plain of York, with its magnificent bridges over Tyne and Tweed, and its beautiful trains. The North Eastern trains were unexceptionally good to look at and to travel upon. Just before the 1914 war, the company had the fastest booking in the British Empire. This was the Darlington-York run of the 12.20 p.m. Newcastle-Sheffield express, 43 minutes for the $44\frac{1}{8}$ miles, or $61 \cdot 57$ m.p.h. On February 4, 1911, it made the start-to-stop run in 41 minutes,

64·57 m.p.h., and on another occasion a pass-to-pass average of 68·5 m.p.h. was recorded over 36 miles. The timekeeping of this train was once described as "almost monotonous in its excellence." This was the North Eastern's show train, but it was no light shining in isolated splendour. A most creditable feature of the North Eastern was the noteworthy number of fast local expresses. Where many companies would run an occasional semi-fast, more semi than fast, the North Eastern ran trains which it officially designated express, and express they were. A cross-country journey from Leeds to Northallerton could be a most lively experience. As mentioned, the carriages were consistently good; in this respect the North Eastern branch train from Harrogate to Pateley Bridge was above comparison with a Manchester to Blackpool express on the Lancashire and Yorkshire.

Journeys on the North Eastern were of extraordinary variety. North Eastern trains gave you the finest of all views to be had of Durham—seen at its best about sunrise—from them you saw the Tyne as it should be seen; you saw a magical glimpse of the Farne Islands; you saw, and never forgot, the Whitby and Pickering line. There were those lovely branches up the Yorkshire dales, to Richmond, to Masham, and up the Nidd Valley; there was the solemn journey over the Pennines on what had been the westward extension of the Stockton and Darlington Railway, with its magnificent viaducts; there was the Newcastle and Carlisle line, leading you from the grim backs of Scotswood, past the cottage where George Stephenson was born at Wylam, and away over the wild rainy hills where the Pennines end and the Cheviots begin. Finally, the North Eastern was the only English railway which succeeded in crossing the border into Scotland. It ran a service to Kelso on the North British and served Carham and Sprouston Stations north of the border. It also served Coldstream, but though the village was in Scotland, the station was across the bridge, with the Sunday beer, in England. Out of respect, perhaps, for the Kirk Sessions, the North Eastern ran no Sunday trains on its Kelso branch. North Eastern trains, however, went much farther into Scotland than to Kelso; through most of the company's history, it worked the Anglo-Scottish East Coast expresses through to Edinburgh with its own engine power. Once only was there a break in this tradition. The story of what happened, however, belongs more conveniently to the North British part of our narrative. It was a very jolly quarrel from the outside observers' point of view.

Really, for a railway that made a large proportion of its living out of coal, iron ore and shipping—it was the largest dock-owner of all the old companies, the North Eastern did its passengers extraordinarily well. Even purely local services were livened up by what were sportily called autocars—actually an old Fletcher 0–4–4 tank engine working push-and-pull with one or two clerestory bogie carriages—Newcastle-upon-Tyne had a most creditable electric suburban service as far back as 1902, before anything of the kind had been attempted by any main-line railway company elsewhere. The first above-ground electric railway in Great Britain, and also the first elevated electric railway in the world, was the Liverpool Overhead, with its grand scenic tour of the Merseyside docks, opened over part of its route in 1893, only three years after the City and South London, the first electric tube in the world.

With the North Eastern we come to the end of the old English main-line railways. Before going over the Border into Scotland, we should take a retrospect of the Welsh railways, all of them small, but several of first-rate importance. With the Welsh railways it was difficult to decide when a local railway did not come within the main-line category. But then, in England this was not easy; I have probably got into trouble already with irate readers for thus dignifying the Maryport and Carlisle, but not the Cleator and Workington Junction.

Down in the great coal-bearing valleys of South Wales there was a dense network of railways, fated in the end to fall into the Great Western net, but in our time worked by numerous, highly individual companies that competed with one another in the most energetic manner. The Taff Vale had only 124 miles of route, but its traffic was relatively tremendous. At Pontypridd it dealt with 500 trains daily; it had about 250 locomotives, largely 0–6–2 coal tanks; its two and a half thousand goods and mineral wagons were but a drop in the ocean of privately-owned colliery vehicles which it handled; it owned the Penarth docks and their railway system. Heavily graded on its main lines, it had, on a mineral line at Blaenclydach, a really spectacular gradient, half a mile at 1 in 13, whereon the locomotives were assisted by stationary haulage with an endless rope. These locomotives themselves, three special 0–6–0 side tanks, were out of the ordinary. The firebox crown was sloped, so that it would remain covered with water on the steep gradient; above it was a large dome, giving the engine a somewhat archaic appearance. In addition to the usual appliances, skid brakes were provided, acting on the rails like the magnetic brakes on a tram.

Predominantly a goods line as it was, the Taff Vale worked a quite creditable passenger service. Its chief mechanical engineer, T. Hurry Riches, a stern, imposing character with a goatee beard, designed for it in 1888 some very handsome 4–4–2 tank engines, which were the Taff Vale's nearest approach to an express passenger clan. They were the first British inside-cylinder engines of this type, taken up by many railways in later years. One of them, No. 173, caused the Llantrissant smash of August 12, 1893, by dropping a broken spring under her own train, going down from Merthyr to Cardiff. A single hidden flaw in one of the spring hangers thus had excessively spectacular results, attended, unfortunately, by much loss of life. Apart from this sad occasion they were admirable engines, and very elegant in their original red livery with polished domes and chimney caps.

Unlike those of many lines catering chiefly for industrial needs, the Taff Vale carriages were excellent of their kind. They were, furthermore, embellished with a delightfully zoological coat of arms. For the crest there was a goat, a suave, gentlemanly goat. Below him, enclosed in a garter, was the Welsh national dragon. The late E. L. Ahrons wrote: "I hope that the real Welsh dragon is of more respectable appearance.

The Taff Vale variety—genus *Draco Tonypandiensis*—is a dancing, shrieking, riotous beast, engaged in putting out his tongue at the goat and doing his utmost to disturb the stately serenity of the latter." He concluded by suggesting the replacement of the dragon by a more decorous Welsh rabbit.*

The Rhymney Railway had only 50½ miles of route, but here again there was a very heavy traffic, handled by some 120 locomotives. In these it was typified by saddle-tanks with double frames. In the second half of the last century, the Rhymney Railway was Mr. Cornelius Lundie, and Mr. Cornelius Lundie was the Rhymney Railway. An autocrat of the inimitable Victorian stamp, he was pre-eminent of his kind. Cornelius Lundie was general manager. He was also chief engineer, locomotive superintendent, and superintendent of the line. When at last he was induced to retire, he continued to serve the company on the Board, and to boss all departments very much as before. This veteran was one of the last living people to have known Sir Walter Scott, with whom he once lunched at Abbotsford. He was down at the company's offices, taking a director's functions literally, a few days before his death in 1908.

The Barry Railway, with 68 miles of route, was a relative newcomer, its first section having been opened in 1889, and connected Barry Dock with the Rhondda, with through passenger services to the Great Western, Rhymney and Taff Vale lines. It owned, as its name suggests, the huge Barry docks, including 25,850 feet of quays and 108 miles of sidings. From our present point of view one of its claims to interest was its possession of the first o–8–o main-line goods engines in Great Britain, certain of which had previously seen service in Lapland. They were part of an order for the unlucky Swedish and Norwegian Railway in 1886. The Barry acquired the first two in 1889 when it started business. Though built in Glasgow by Sharp Stewart, their outside cylinders and long-roofed cabs gave them a Continental appearance.

* *The Railway Magazine*, October 1922, in the course of the best description of Victorian railway working ever written.

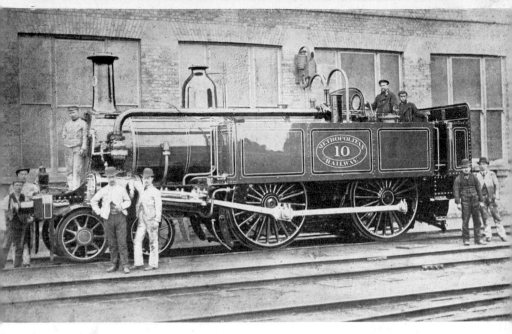

The Metropolitan Classic: Beyer Peacock condensing tank engine No. 10 (originally *Cerberus*), built in 1864, reboilered by Hanbury in 1887

[*London Transport Records*]

North London Railway standard tank engine No. 13, designed by William Adams, modified by J. C. Park, in Broad Street Station

[*Locomotive and General Railway Photographs*]

Our engineers are now engaged upon the Preliminary Work in connection with the construction of UNDERGROUND ELECTRIC RAILWAYS in London, and their special experience in this department will be of immense value in obtaining Electric Railway Contracts.

## POPULARITY OF THE NEW UNDERGROUND

London's latest novelty and its advantages

"No fewer than 84,500 passengers had sampled the new line on its opening day. Thousands more had looked on.

"As the line is open seven days a week, these numbers, if regarded as average traffic figures, would mean a yearly passenger return of 30,000,000 "

*Daily Mail*, August 1, 1900.

"Meantime London, all agape, crowds to the Twopenny Tube. Thursday's traffic completely eclipsed the previous days, as the following list shows:

| | Passengers |
|---|---|
| Monday . . . | 83,000 |
| Tuesday . . . | 91,000 |
| Wednesday . . | 86,000 |
| Thursday . . | 93,000 |

"Yesterday the crowds swayed and surged to get on to the trains. It was a cosmopolitan throng. Nearly every civilized nation under the sun was represented among the humanity that was struggling to experience London's latest sensation."

*Daily Mail*, August 4, 1900

"When a place is Royally opened it is not always really opened. A week or two back the Prince of Wales inaugurated the Central London Railway, but not till yesterday was it available to the public. Not till yesterday, therefore, could expectation be confirmed by experience. It was. The railway is a valuable acquisition to London."

*Daily News*, July 31, 1900

Twopenny Tube: A contemporary artist's impression of the Central London Railway in 1900, with a caricature of one of the original double-bogie locomotives

*[London Transport Records]*

wn Yarmouth express climbing Brentod bank, Great tern Railway, gust 6, 1910 hauled 4–4–0 locomotive 1813 painted grey

[*K. A. C. R. Nunn*]

King's Lynn, Great stern Railway : W. Worsdell comand No. 0706 beside little private engine zelle, which later nt to the Shropshire l Montgomeryshire Railway

*Locomotive and General Railway Photographs*]

e famous experital Decapod No. designed for J. den by Fred V. ssell, Great Eastern Railway

[*F. Moore's Railway Photographs*]

A study in coaching stock: South Eastern Railway officers' special in Folkestone Warren, March 9, 1877, following clearance of a severe chalk slip

[Southern Railway Records]

Brass and Birdcage: One of Harry Wainwright's 4–4–0 express engines in the original exuberant livery of the South Eastern and Chatham Railway, with some typical main-line coaches

[*F. Moore's Railway Photographs*]

Down Continental Express near Bickley, London, Chatham and Dover Railway, hauled by William Kirtley's bogie engine No. 12. The site is that of the present Chislehurst and Bickley Junctions, the South Eastern overbridge being just visible in the background

[*T. F. Budden*]

Rivals at Pompey: Dugald Drummond's No. 292, class C8, London and South Western Railway, and Stroudley's *Cleveland*, Gladstone class, London, Brighton and South Coast Railway, at Portsmouth Harbour

[*O. J. Morris Collection*]

Train from Ryde at Newport, Isle of Wight Central Railway, headed by Beyer Peacock 2–4–0 tank engine No. 5

[*H. Gordon Tidey*]

Up West of England Express, London and South Western Railway: Drummond
T 9 4–4–0 No. 122, with invalid saloon, probably from Sidmouth, next to tender

[*Locomotive and General Railway Photographs*]

Down Bournemouth Express, London and South Western Railway, passing
Surbiton: Drummond "Paddlebox" four-cylinder 4–6–0 No. 447; Salisbury train
approaching on down slow road

Victoria – Eastbourne express passing Balham Intermediate Box, London, Brighton and South Coast Railway, hauled by Marsh Atlantic No. 40 (first series, unsuperheated); the leading vehicle is one of the "Pullman Pup" lighting vans, followed by two American Pullman Cars

[F. Moore's Railway Photographs]

Mighty midgets in Wales included the Cardiff Railway, with less than 12 miles of route, but 135 miles counting its dock lines, and the colossally-named Alexandra (Newport and South Wales) Docks and Railway, with $9\frac{1}{4}$ miles of first track and about 100 miles of dock lines. In the midst of its more serious business, it contrived to work a passenger service, for which it provided four carriages. There were thirty-eight engines and a large fleet of wagons, though, like its neighbours, it carried most of its traffic in private owners' wagons.

From the turmoil of the dock-owning railways one could turn to the rurality, even the remoteness of the Neath and Brecon, with its ancient carriages bought second-hand from the North London and the South Western, and, among others, a shapely little 4-4-0 tank engine which also contrived to look like the North London at its brightest, though it was designed and built new for the N. and B. Of more heavy calibre was the Brecon and Merthyr, which provided a link between the congested south and the wilder hills of Central Wales. Like the Rhymney, it was addicted to six-coupled saddle tank engines, which toiled pluckily up the mountainous main line—up and down, rather, for that line was something like railways of a less serious type at Blackpool, Southend, etc.—between Brecon and Newport. Working the heavy coal trains over a route where gradients of 1 in 38 to 1 in 40 went on for miles was a ticklish business at the best of times, and there were one or two spectacular occasions on which those trains ran away with their locomotives and did a good deal of damage. This railway, too, received very engaging treatment by Ahrons in the series mentioned, including a racy account of a prayer meeting held on his behalf by a party of Welsh evangelists in a Brecon and Merthyr third-class smoker, which meeting came to a premature end when one of the two engines on the train developed violent valve trouble going up Torpantau Bank, opening vistas of an abrupt return down the back with Eternity at the bottom. "The gentleman who had shown so much solicitude for my future welfare was obviously ill at ease. Now that it had come to the point that there was even a bare suggestion of his having to leave this bad and sinful world for a better one, he did not appear to be in any very great hurry to quit."*

As mentioned, there were dozens of fascinating railways in Wales; Burry Port and Gwendreath Valley, Llanelly and Mynydd Mawr—in the hands of a capable bard their very names could be made into real poetry. But having got to the Brecon and Merthyr, present limitations oblige us to follow its lovely northern section to join the Cambrian in the magnificent Central Wales route ending on the Cambrian main line at Moat Lane Junction, one of the most gorgeous railway rides in the world, and to this day, thank heavens, one of the slowest.

The Cambrian was the largest of the old Welsh Railways, and it was also the only one that operated anything resembling a fast main-line service, carrying through traffic off the Great Western and London and North Western systems to the coast towns of Cardigan Bay. For a company never counted among the wealthy, it yet provided, like the Midland and South Western Junction, some extremely creditable trains. It even had two admirable observation cars on the coast section, which it had economically converted from two old composite carriages. They had large windows all round and small reversible seats; few could guess that quite a large part of the original bodies, as well as the underframes, was retained.

At the end of our period, the Cambrian had 300 miles of route, including lines worked, yet it had only 100 locomotives compared with the Taff Vale's 257. The older engines, built by Sharp Stewart, were in many cases identical with those of the Furness Railway. In addition to the observation cars mentioned, there were some delightful composite carriages in which the end compartments had windows on three sides and, on the outer side, a pair of neat armchairs in place of the ordinary high-back seats. In the course of through running, these naturally turned up on the Great Western, which admired them so much that it copied them in some non-corridor composites built at the beginning of this century.

This is not supposed to be a chronicle of railway accidents,

* *The Railway Magazine*, August 1922.

though several seem to have found their way in already, and one cannot consider the Cambrian without noticing something very curious which recurred on Y Vriog incline, that dizzy terrace along the cliffs going down to Barmouth from the Dovey Junction direction. On the evening of January 1, 1883, a rock-fall occurred in front of a down train from Machynlleth to Barmouth at the northern end of Y Vriog. The engine *Pegasus*, a standard 2–4–0 of the period, mounted the obstruction and went over the cliff, killing her driver and fireman. The thing became a queer tragedy of the past. Fifty years rolled by and the Cambrian had become a Great Western constituent. Then in the grey dawn of March 4, 1933, the stone pitching supporting the main coast road went thundering down the cliff on to the railway. This time it was the mail train, hauled by 0–6–0 No. 874 (old Cambrian No. 54), that ran into the obstruction. Over went the engine and tender with the enginemen, to fall 80 ft. on to the rocks below. The engine was smashed to pieces and again both men were killed. There is now an elaborate system of avalanche tunnels in the danger zone.

The Cambrian was noteworthy for the possession or working of several most interesting minor railways. There were the narrow-gauge Vale of Rheidol and the Welshpool and Llanfair lines, and, by lease, the unique Van Railway, connecting the Van leadmines with the Cambrian at Caersws. Opened on August 14, 1871, it had a very brief career as a passenger-carrying line, lasting as such only from 1873, when two old carriages were moved in, to 1879, though it carried goods until late in 1940. In its early days, it was surely the only railway to have a bard for its general manager, in the person of John Ceiriog Hughes, who was a celebrated figure in the history of Celtic poetry. A surviving portrait shows him as a most druidical looking old gentleman posed before an ash tree.

# CHAPTER FOUR

# THE SCOTTISH COMPANIES

THIS is an honest book. It began by showing its author's favour for the London and South Western, and now it brings him to the greatest of his acquired tastes. That is for the railways of Scotland, and for the noble—sometimes poor but always proud—trains that ran upon them.

It was a natural love at first sight, uninfluenced by Scots parentage on the distaff side. In the first five minutes that I spent afoot on Scottish soil, I was engaged in an energetic argument with an incredulous parent, that the engine before us, at Hawick on the North British, was like one on the London and South Western. Of course it was; Dugald Drummond had designed it. Moreover, the first Highland engine I saw, in a pearly mountain dawn at Kingussie, was almost a South Western T 9 4–4–0. Whatever it might have lost with six inches off the coupled wheels it gained by the glorious possession of a sonorous Gaelic name. To my shame I forget that name, but it was *Ben* Something. A little later I knew them all from No. 1, *Ben-y-Gloe* to No. 47, *Ben a' Bhuird*.

Peter Drummond had designed them, or, more nearly, had looked over his brother's shoulder and carefully copied. These little Bens were most pretty engines. But Peter Drummond's best locomotives were the 4–6–0 Castles, first built in 1900, of which he designed the tenders. His predecessor at Inverness, David Jones, had designed though not built the engines, to which were added the Drummond family chimney and cab. Of course nobody mentioned it in Britain, at any rate in print, though in America Angus Sinclair wrote fairly freely. Whatever their parentage, I enjoyed the Highland locomotives, so much so that I wrote a history of them when I was supposed to be reading for my Schools. It was not a good history, and I got what I deserved on its account, but that did not interfere with the thrill I feel to this day when the north-bound train swings away round the curve from Stanley Junction and faces the great hills.

Largest of the Scottish railways, and a partner in two of the three Anglo-Scottish main lines, was the North British. It was not the best of the Scotch companies; as already suggested, its local trains were deplorable, and even the expresses were patchy in the quality of their rolling stock, but in spite of these things, and of its miserable stations in Glasgow, the North British was a highly imposing concern. As operator, and a partner in the jointly-owned Forth Bridge Railway, it presented to public admiration the world's grandest example of civil engineering. To this day the Forth Bridge is a superb thing, whether seen distantly against sunrise, or close at hand, straddling the sky. At night, with the glare from an open fire-door striking upwards to the topmost girders, it has an awful beauty. My first journey over the Forth Bridge was in a train of bumping six-wheel coaches with a peculiar smell about them, drawn by an old Holmes 4-4-0 engine with a small Drummondian boiler and a Stirling cab, its pea-soup paint none too clean. That was somehow characteristic of the North British; the poor and the magnificent were ever side-by-side. You could sit in an admirable Aberdeen express in the great Waverley Station at Edinburgh, looking across the platform at the stopping train to Hyndland via Bathgate, and wonder why people ever made rude remarks concerning the South Eastern.

In 1914 the North British Railway had 1,393 miles of route open, extending from Hexham in Northumberland and Silloth in Cumberland to Edinburgh, Glasgow, Perth, Dundee, and, by running powers over the Caledonian north of Kinnaber Junction, to Aberdeen. In the west, it took in the spectacular West Highland Railway and the Invergarry and Fort Augustus Railway up the Great Glen, forming, in part, links in what was very nearly a Glasgow and North Western Railway to Inverness. The Mallaig extension of the West Highland, following the old Road to the Isles by Ailort and Morar, is a line to which only the Highland run from about the middle of Glen Carron to the Kyle of Lochalsh is comparable. In its earliest days, the West Highland line had special rolling stock built for it by the North British—centre-corridor saloon coaches designed to show off the scenery to their passengers— far, far superior to the sort of thing provided for mere business expresses between Glasgow or Edinburgh and Aberdeen.

The older North British locomotives were a collective marvel, indeed, the stock inherited by Dugald Drummond in the 'seventies beggared description. Before him, Wheatley had made some attempt to standardize, but on a small scale only. Express engines were few, and with good reason; in the early 'seventies, with the Forth and Tay Bridges unbuilt, the Midland route to Scotland uncompleted, and the North Eastern working the East Coast expresses to Edinburgh, there was precious little for an express locomotive to do on the North British. The fast Edinburgh and Glasgow trains were worked by pretty little Beyer Peacock single-wheelers which had belonged to the formerly independent Edinburgh and Glasgow Railway. They were among the best of the old brigade; Wheatley began rebuilding them and Drummond completed the job. They ended their days after very long careers around half a century, the last survivor being No. 1006 (old No. 216), built in 1861 and withdrawn in 1912, having completed her life on the Border Counties line between Riccarton and Hexham.

Of some dozens of miscellaneous antiques, we should notice two in particular. One was No. 55. This began as a solitary Crampton stern-wheeler in 1848. In 1850 she hauled the royal train to Edinburgh when Queen Victoria opened the Royal Border Bridge, for which auspicious occasion she (the engine) was decorated with the Stewart dress tartan (presumably in a panel; a Crampton painted all over in that most showy of tartans beats credulity!). In 1865, by a very severe operation, she was rebuilt as a 2–2–2 instead of a 4–2–0. In 1897 Matthew Holmes gave her a second-hand Drummond boiler of vintage 1877. She lasted ten years longer, one of her haunts being the leisurely line from Ladybank Junction to Perth.

If No. 55 was a quiet and gentle old lady of an engine, No. 38 was far otherwise, dubious of origin, great in reputation, a veritable Sappho among locomotives. Tom Wheatley built her in 1869 out of scrap and odd spare parts; Holmes gave her a more modern boiler in 1893; she was put on to the fast business trains between Balloch and Bridgeton Cross, and she proceeded to sparkle as perhaps no suburban locomotive has ever done before or since. The Dumbarton and Balloch line was joint between North British and Caledonian. Each company ran a fast morning business train to Glasgow, and officially they left Balloch at the same time. As this, of course, was physically impossible on a single up road, the two companies had a gentlemen's agreement that each should start its train first on alternate weeks. At Dumbarton, their lines separated, running roughly parallel along the banks of the Clyde and crossing at different levels. The Caledonian train made an additional stop at Dumbarton East for Denny's shipyards, and on days when it started first, this enabled the North British train to catch it up, after which there was a glorious race from Dumbarton to Clydebank, with a final crossing near Partick. For much of the way the trains were in sight of one another and the sporting feelings of the two sets of passengers ran high. If you were betting against the North British, and No. 38 was on its train, you could write that off, for she was inevitably away down the course by the time the Caledonian reached Bowling.

North British No. 38, latterly bearing the duplicate number 1126, lasted until 1913. Her anatomy was supposed to contain parts of an engine dating back to 1847, an old Hawthorn single bearing the same number but otherwise not the slightest resemblance to this resolute double-framed 2–4–0. For one of the accompanying plates I have painted her in her best-known guise, with the 1893 boiler and the olive-green livery of that time. Thoroughly unconventional engine that she was, at one period she was painted yellow while the tender, a standard Wheatley six-wheeler, was green, doubtless having been purloined from a goods engine.

In 1871, before Drummond's advent, Wheatley built two locomotives, Nos. 224 and 264, which were the first British standard gauge inside-framed, inside-cylinder express locomotives, soon fated to become an absolute national type. By chance, No. 224 became notorious for quite another reason. At the end of 1879 she was the spare engine at Dundee. On December 28th, the regular engine for the Sunday mail train down to Burntisland and back, Drummond 0-4-2 tank *Ladybank*, broke down. Consequently it was No. 224 that hauled the train, and just after 7.0 p.m. she went down with the first Tay Bridge in one of the greatest railway disasters in history. Later, in the spring of 1880, engine and tender were recovered. The chimney, cab and dome casing had gone, but essentially No. 224 was little the worse for wear; last rebuilt in 1897, she ran until 1919.

Later North British locomotives were eminently respectable. The big Atlantics built from 1907 onwards were among the most imposing engines in the country when they first came out; admirable were the Scotts—*Rob Roy*, *The Fair Maid*, *Adam Woodcock*, and the rest—which only now, at the time of writing, are beginning to go the way of all scrap. But we are not done with oddities; the North British abounded in them.

Up till 1907, the show-piece among peculiar features of operation was the Cowlairs incline out of Queen Street, Glasgow. As at Blaenclydach on the Taff Vale, locomotives were assisted up the bank by an endless wire rope, worked by a large Neilson stationary engine at the top. A messenger rope connected the hauling cable to an inverted drawhook on the buffer beam, off which it automatically dropped when the train topped the bank and gained on the stationary engine. Downgoing trains were given a robust push from the rear and went solemnly engineless to Queen Street, headed by several special brake wagons.

The North Eastern's running powers into Edinburgh, which were balanced by North British running powers over the

North Eastern from Hexham to Newcastle, and under which all the best trains from Berwick to the capital were worked by the North Eastern, resulted, as already mentioned, in a first-class row in the 'nineties. The North British suddenly decided to evict the North-Eastern, and during long wrangles which were dragged into the House of Lords, gave them notice to clear out. Having put the Allies in their place, the North British was in honour bound to bring the trains into Edinburgh without loss of time, in spite of the extra stop for changing engines at Berwick. The Lords washed their hands of the business and told the disputants that they had better call in the Railway Commission. The North Eastern duly departed under protest, in 1897, and the North British proceeded to carry out its obligations. North of Berwick the East Coast expresses were now hauled by N.B.R. locomotives, usually working in pairs to guard against failures, which they did very creditably. Matthew Holmes's 633 class, designed in 1891, were usually employed, though sometimes the old Drummond veterans did turns. Two of these blotted the North British copy-book on one occasion by running at full speed into the back of a goods train at Prestonpans, but all round, the North British locomotive department did its part nobly, and some very fine locomotive work resulted from this memorable quarrel. It came to an end in the beginning of 1898, when the Railway Commission gave its ruling, as a result of which the North Eastern returned to work some, though not quite all of the Anglo-Scottish expresses.

Before leaving this brief sketch of a not impeccable, but undoubtedly great Scottish railway, we should recall an old-age exploit of one of the Drummond express engines, No. 487 (originally *Montrose*, renamed *Waverley* after the fall of the old Tay Bridge, which caused her transference from the Aberdeen road to the Waverley route). Summoned to England by an urgent telegram one day in 1916, a soldier was too late to catch the 10.30 a.m. Midland Scotch express from the Waverley, and chartered a special to catch it up at Carlisle. The train consisted of No. 487 and a single Midland coach, and it covered the 98 miles, 15 chains, in 105 minutes, including a dead stand of one minute at Abbeyhill, a signal check just north of Hawick and a four minutes stop there, and a slack owing to engineering repairs between Scotch Dyke and Longtown. Allowing for these stops and checks, the journey was made at a mile a minute throughout, and though a single Midland coach did not make much of a load (25 tons) this was a most remarkable performance for so old an engine over such a road. The passenger made his connection at Carlisle through the express being held five minutes for him.

For all their faults, the North British trains were favourites of mine, and it is therefore without prejudice that I now describe those of the Caledonian Railway as the finest and most imposing of aspect on any British railway in the old days. A Caledonian express, with its massive blue engine and its carriages of red-brown and white was a superb sight, whether it were toiling up from Beattock to the summit through the great bare hills that stretch from Wamphray to Tinto, or racing through the green Carse of Gowrie with the Highland hills blue on the northern skyline, over that stretch from Forfar to Perth which for a while saw the fastest regular run in the country, or toiling doggedly through the Pass of Brander below Ben Cruachan, snow-flecked blue in the spring sunshine, where an elaborate system of wires and automatic signals gave warning of any boulders that might happen to fall on to the line.

The Caledonian was recognizable in the dark. Going north by the West Coast route at night, you could not suddenly wake up in a close-curtained sleeper and mistake Carlisle for Wigan. Up at the front you heard the voice of the new engine which had just come on, so different from the eldritch North Western shriek, a deep hoot as of a loud bassoon. England knows it now, for years after the passing of the Caley, the L.M.S. revived and standardized that admirable whistle. It was more of the influential Dugald Drummond's work, modelled by him on the whistles of the Clyde steamers. John McIntosh's great 4–6–0 engine *Cardean*, which for long invariably took over the 2.0 p.m. Scotch express from Euston at Carlisle, had, however, a particular whistle, modelled more on that of a Cunard liner. You could recognize *Cardean* miles away down the valley of the Annan. At both Carlisle and Glasgow Central, she had her regular fans who gathered to see her off again and again; Driver Gibson was a popular hero—almost a demigod to boys, who used to speculate on whether the two brilliant coins mounted, amid elaborate brazen filigree, on her regulator, were bright ha'pennies or in very truth sovereigns, and to fanatics the former suggestion was not in entirely good taste.

Many of the best trains were usually hauled by big 4–4–0 engines, the third enlargement of McIntosh's famous *Dunalastair* of 1896. The twelve-wheel "Grampian" corridor carriages used on the crack Aberdeen expresses were comparable with the best stock on the North Western and the Midland, and caused you to forgive the Caley for the scruffy vehicles which it inflicted on some of its local trains (three inches of stale rain and the corpses of half-a-dozen flies in the lamp globe). Yet even those Caledonian locals had an air about them; the Ballachulish branch train, hauled by an ancient Oban Bogie 4–4–0 or a diminutive 0–4–4 tank, as splendidly blue as their big sisters, rumbling over Connel Ferry's great bridge, then under the rock of Dun Balanrigh and northwards to the foot of Glencoe, had great prestige in its own country. Fussing northwards in the morning it became the Mail, and the Loch Linnhe villages turned out to see it.

Then there was the special inspection train. Sooner or later it would turn up on every line, however remote. It consisted of the tall single driver No. 123 (built by Neilson for the Edinburgh Exhibition of 1886 and used, two years later, in the Race to the North), hauling a single saloon coach. That coach was a work of art. It had been built, about the turn of the century, nominally as an observation car, but apparently the Caledonian officers liked it so much that it was appropriated for departmental use only.

At the end of 1914 the Caledonian Railway had just under 1,118 miles of route. It worked the 100-mile Callander and Oban Railway with its spectacular transit of the Perthshire and Argyllshire Highlands, as well as some less imposing but sometimes more remunerative lines such as the Cathcart District in Glasgow. Both the Caledonian and the North British operated underground lines in Glasgow, the Glasgow Central and the Glasgow City and District respectively. Of these fuming burrows, the less said the better. Unelectrified, they have grown old in sin. While we are presently concerned with trains, it should be recalled that unlike so many British railways, the Caledonian was at pains to make its stations as attractive as possible. Even some of the most unpromising places were gentled in condition by the bright geranium basket; in a country of dour architecture the stations of the Caledonian—indeed many stations on all five Scottish railways —had an agreeable quality of mellow stone walls and corbiestepped gables. In the Highlands, and particularly on the Callander and Oban line, there were some really delightful platform gardens, often adorned with fountain or natural cascade.

Like the Midland, and in collaboration with it, the Glasgow and South Western Railway assumed importance as part of a through Anglo-Scottish route at the beginning of our period. To a visitor from the south, seeing it for the first time, it suggested the South Eastern Railway in the aspect of its locomotives, just as the North British, and to a lesser extent the Highland, suggested the London and South Western. Both the famous Stirling brothers had been in command of its locomotive department, and until James Manson came in the late 'nineties, the domeless boiler was supreme. The celebrated Stirling locomotives of the Great Northern (Patrick Stirling) and the South Eastern (James Stirling) had their ancestors on the Glasgow and South Western, and for long after the Stirling period Hugh Smellie perpetuated many Stirling features in locomotive design. Some of James Stirling's magnificent 4–4–0 seven-footers had extraordinarily long careers; the last of them were finally broken up by the London Midland and Scottish in the nineteen-thirties.

In other respects, Glasgow and South Western trains did not resemble those of the South Eastern; their carriages were on the whole very much better, and some of them were really excellent. The Sou'-West did not exhibit such spectacular examples of fast running as the Caledonian or, in England, the North Eastern and the Great Western, but there were some remarkably smart timings over the hilly route from Glasgow to Carlisle, and with the Irish boat trains from Glasgow to Stranraer over that nightmare route from Girvan to Portpatrick. For details of this, of the engines that worked them, and above all the enginemen, readers are referred to the delightful articles by David L. Smith in the *Railway Magazine* and *The Locomotive* during recent years, wherein one may come to know, as if by personal introduction, such characters as The Mool and The Calculator. Scotland is a country of nicknames, but those of the Sou'-West enginemen were of surpassing richness, like Mr. Smith's anecdotes.

The Glasgow and South Western and the Caledonian were usually at point of dirk; a Sou'-West engineman would believe anything, however heinous, however dastardly, of a Caledonian man; how the Portpatrick and Wigtownshire Joint Railway was worked without frequent bloodshed passes comprehension. Down in Galloway there was once a head-on collision on single track between trains of both companies; so long as old Glasgow and South Western men survive it will be told how one of the Caledonian enginemen mounted the Sou'-West engine while its driver and fireman were helpless, and tried to cook the evidence by stealing the train staff.

Among its enginemen, the Glasgow and South Western had a ballad-singer, a true son of ancient Scots minstrelsy. The moon of his delight was not some blue-eyed lass of Corkerhill nor yet the fine red-haired barmaid at St. Enoch; she was Stirling 0–4–2 mixed-traffic engine No. 259:—

> She was built by Dübs and Company
> In eighteen-seventy-six,
> For either goods or passenger;
> She's one that never sticks.

She runs along so smooth and clean,
　　Always up to time;
She's a gallant little masterpiece,
　　Two–five–nine!*

Not exemplary rhyming, but with a quality of sincerity lacking in many works technically more correct. There was a lot of it, and at the end, of course, *We beat the Caledonian with the Two-five-nine*. Those old Stirling mixed-traffics, like the seven-footers, lasted for many years, a few into the nineteen-thirties. Under James Manson, the locomotive department of the Glasgow and South Western was as nearly a happy family as a locomotive department can be. He was a most kind and charming man, the antithesis of the harsh and bullying Dugald Drummond, and he approached locomotive design and management like an artist. The finest Lucca olive oil was used on the Pullman engines in Manson's day.

This most worthy engineer first made his mark, before coming to the Glasgow and South Western, on the Great North of Scotland Railway, where he devised the apparatus for exchanging tablets at full speed on single-line sections. Moreover, he refused to claim his patent royalties, on the grounds that such an arrangement should be free to all users for humanitarian reasons.

At the beginning of our period, the Great North of Scotland was one of the worst railways in Great Britain; its train services were vile, its treatment of passengers arbitrary, its relations with its neighbours—the Caledonian and the Highland—extremely hostile, at the special expense of anybody who wanted to catch a Great North connection. It competed with the South Eastern and the Lancashire and Yorkshire in general evil-doing, and beat them hollow. Then, like the Lanky, it reformed its ways, though it did this thing even better, for about the regenerate Scotch railway there was none of the severe rectitude and efficient ugliness that spoiled the English company in its better days. Though, in spite of its name, it was the smallest Scottish railway, with 334½ miles open in 1914

* Acknowledgement to Malcolm Niven.

compared with 491½ on the Glasgow and South Western and 492¼ on the Highland, it had in general the smartest, cleanest and most comfortable trains in Scotland. The engines were small—the largest, little 4–4–0's—and the loads were generally light, but they provided a most convenient and snappy service. The suburban trains from Aberdeen to Culter and Dyce, often quite heavily loaded and hauled by 0–4–4 tank engines, should have been a lesson to more than one of the railways serving the London area. Some of the stations, such as Elgin, and certain of those on the Deeside line to Ballater, were outstanding.

In the flush of its renaissance, the Great North showed signs of branching out into a much bigger railway, with a long mountain line over the Grampians by Tomintoul to Inverness and thence, partly by running powers over the Highland Railway, to the far North-West.

The Highland Railway, of course, had other intentions; indeed, it was owing to Great North ambitions that the Highland pushed through the long-delayed short cut from Aviemore to Inverness over Slochd Mhuic Pass, eliminating the old, long hike over Dava Moor and round by Forres and Nairn. Twice the Highland was threatened with an attack on its monopoly of Inverness; the other possibility was that proposed Glasgow and North Western Railway running northwards from Loch Lomond through the mountains and then up the Great Glen, mentioned in connection with the West Highland line of the North British.

So the Great North was kept more or less in its place, which some people, who used the Highland regularly, thought a pity. It settled down, however, to a very respectable existence in its own territory, consisting of north-eastern Scotland level with and above Aberdeen, extending westwards to Ballater, Boat of Garten and Elgin. A hint of the old fighting spirit survived in a crafty notice-board of immense size, which it mounted on a shed at Boat of Garten where passengers on the Highland Railway could see it, suggesting to them that the proper thing for them to do if they were bound for the south was to get out, shake the Highland dust from their shoes, and board the Speyside branch train of the Great North which might await them on the other side of the island platform.

In general, however, the Great North came to be on very good terms with its friends at Inverness. Really admirable corridor expresses were run between Aberdeen and Inverness, both companies providing the motive power and each working right through from city to city. Then, in the summer, the Great North used to provide the most admirable scenic excursions from Aberdeen to Speyside, through Dufftown and Glen Fiddich to that beautiful branch running south-west from Craigellachie along the banks of Spey to Grantown and The Boat. I might say, with many: "What a grand line the Great North would have been had it reached Inverness!" But I liked the Highland, and knew it first.

Jokes were made about the Highland, in Scotland, just as they were about the South Eastern in English comic papers. You heard, until you were sick of it, about the Highland mail train from Inverness which reached Helmsdale twelve hours late and, when it finally arrived at Wick, was mistaken for the next day's mail running to time. With really bad snow conditions in winter or early spring, trains could be later than that, and small blame to those who tried to keep the line clear about that desolate county march between Sutherland and Caithness. I have often known the north mail train to be several hours late in summer, and it was usually found that this abysmal unpunctuality had its origins south of Perth, even on the great and complacent London and North Western. Things are not likely to improve when a service has to be run over several hundred miles, chiefly single track, with the schedules blown to blazes by other companies' misdeeds. Moreover, during the summer rush, there was a flood of traffic going north and precious little coming south except for such empty stock as could be worked back. Inverness became a resting place for masses of passenger coaches, sleeping cars, saloons, vans and horseboxes, belonging to every British main-line railway. Every Highland locomotive worked overtime,

The Most Memorable Thirty-Eight, North British Railway: here shown coupled to an American Pullman car at Cowlairs. Behind the cab is the ancient signalbox with its clock

whereas during the slack months they numbered rather more than the company needed. They were very good locomotives, and although north of Inverness, and still more north of Dingwall, running was usually of monumental slowness, some very smart work indeed was done on the Inverness-Perth line over the 1,484 ft. summit level of Druimuachdar Pass. It is pleasant indeed to record that the Highland locomotives as a whole were the best of all the Scottish engines taken over by the L.M.S. in 1923, both in condition and in competence for the work they had to do.

One's first view of a Highland train usually contained something out of the ordinary. The Drummond engines we have already noticed, but most characteristic of the old company were those built by David Jones from the 'seventies to the 'nineties. Immediately prominent was the chimney, which had an outer casing like a ship's funnel, in the front of which was a set of louvres designed to cause an updraught through the annular space surrounding the chimney proper. Its object was to prevent the smoke from beating down over the cab when the engine was coasting or running with a bare whiff of steam on the long downhill stretches. The typical Jones engine was a shapely design, with outside cylinders, painted green with a narrow copper cap to the peculiar chimney. Highland passenger engines had territorial names for the most part—Bens, Lochs, Castles, Straths, and the names of the Highland residences of the Company's nabobs: *Auchtertyre, Ballindalloch, Rosehaugh* and the rest. There was also old *Clachnacuddin*, which survived collision with a fallen tree one snowy, windy night at Killiecrankie; she was named after an ancient stone where generations of Inverness washerwomen had been wont to forgather.

The Highland carriages also were often peculiar. They were not exactly luxurious; both first class and third were plainly and severely finished, though saved from the dreariness of the Lancashire and Yorkshire by autumnal-looking patterns in figured plush and moquette. Some of the older carriages had chariot-shaped end compartments, with seats on the inner side only, facing observation windows that gave a fine view of the blind end of the next coach, with mountain scenery thrown in on each side. Two curious short-bodied Pullman sleeping cars, called *Balmoral* and *Dunrobin*, ran on the night trains between Glasgow and Inverness from 1885 to 1907, when the Highland replaced them with composite first-sleeping and third-ordinary carriages of Peter Drummond's design. The "chariot" carriages were the work of David Jones, who built for the company the first British 4–6–0 locomotives in 1894. Except for the through trains from the south, made up of English or joint stock, very few corridor carriages were to be seen on the Highland, and for refreshments, passengers were dependent on station catering. Aviemore, Achmasheen on the Dingwall and Skye line, and Bonar Bridge on the farther north line, had excellent refreshment rooms. An insistent electric bell, in conjunction with an instrument that indicated "Train going North" and "Train going South," agitated the anxious passengers as they milled alongside the bar.

But the breakfast basket service on the night trains was extremely good. Future generations will never know how magically hot bacon and eggs, tea or coffee, and lashings of butter and marmalade could come out of an unpromising-looking basket at Perth, or Kingussie or Inverness. The same applied to Crianlarich, on the N.B.R. West Highland line.

Two of the best trains to give you an introduction to the Highlands were the night train from Perth, conveying a sleeper and through coaches off the Caledonian 10.0 p.m. out of Glasgow, and the late afternoon train from Inverness to the Kyle of Lochalsh. On the night train, in August, the dawn glimmered over the mountains as you climbed solemnly up the Big Hill from Blair Atholl to Druimuachdar summit; going down Strathspey, you saw the sun rise in peerless majesty over the cloudy Cairngorms, where summer snow lay in remote bluish flecks among the high corries, and the whole world sparkled as the train made its second climb to Slochd before running down to Inverness by Tomatin and Culloden with their superb viaducts across the Findhorn and Nairn valleys.

The Skye line from Dingwall, dating from the 'seventies, originally went only as far as Strome-Ferry, a barnlike station on Loch Carron, where militant Calvinism once caused a riot over a Sabbath-breaking fish train, righteous Highlandmen even lying down in front of the offending locomotive and daring the driver to run over them. The line was extended to the Kyle, close to Kyleakin in Skye, in 1897, forming one of the finest pieces of coastwise railway in the world. Unlike some less happy lines in Ireland it is still there; even cars have to be ferried along it by rail, for there is no road from Strathcarron to the Kyle and its ferry.

To me it is best remembered from a stormy summer evening; let me repeat it, for the run is still there to be made, though in a staid and respectable L.M.S. train instead of a string of odd green coaches behind a plucky little Skye Bogie. Crossing the moors in the neighbourhood of Achanalt, the train seems a tiny, toiling thing in a bleak vastitude. Away on one side tumbles the untamed Bran River; around the moors rise great bare hills, here in a splash of golden afternoon sunshine through a rift in the marching clouds, there in inky shade. A peaty pool throws back the vivid blue reflection of a single break. It is there for a moment, then gone for ever. At Achnashellach in Glencarron you are in a howling rainstorm, one of those rapid, drenching storms that beat up a Highland glen, only to leave all sparkling and steaming in a glare of sunshine twenty minutes later. You cannot see the hills, but there is something in that rain-swept Achnashellach that tells you they are all about you and very close.

A sudden brightening makes you look upwards. A vivid blue rift forms in the grey cloud; it widens; for a brief, incredible moment it frames a bare summit, a mountain wet and gleaming in the light of the invisible sun, a mountain poised a-top of you, ready to fall upon the train.

One scene more. Released from the close embrace of the glen, the train is careering joyously along the shores of Loch Carron. Above it on one side, the rocks rise precipitously; there is just room for the railway between their foot and the golden brown sea-wrack. At every other twist of the line, your engine flashes into view, her side rods bravely pounding. On the open side, Loch Carron preserves a surface glassy-smooth; the squall that so lately passed over the waters is forgotten of them. Statuesque herons stand in tiny shallows and gaze sphinxily down into the depths at every promontory. Ahead, the blue hills of Skye— pyramidal Ben na Caillich and the distant, unearthly Cuillin— rise in superb procession. Away to north-west the sun drops in unclouded splendour over Macleod's Table. Eastwards, the storm still rages unrelenting in upper Glen Carron; against a veil of weeping blackness soars a magnificent double rainbow, reflected by the still waters of the loch so that it forms a pair of complete concentric circles, unbelievably vivid. Nearer at hand rise magical rowans, their pale trunks, feathery leaves and masses of scarlet berries standing out, startlingly as the rainbows, against the black of the retreating storm and the deep blue-green of the loch. Hooting merrily, the train gallops on to her goal in the eye of the setting sun.

# CHAPTER FIVE

# THE IRISH COMPANIES

THROUGHOUT our period, of course, all Ireland was Ireland, and although that was a part of the United Kingdom, there was at least no frontier cutting through the main lines of the Great Northern, the Sligo, Leitrim and Northern Counties, the Donegal and the Londonderry and Lough Swilly. These and the others were all Irish railways, and even though the Belfast and Northern Counties Railway became a Midland protectorate, it went on being very much an Irish railway.

Yet perhaps the most Irish of all the Irish railways, at any rate of all the main-line companies, was the Midland Great Western, even though it went nowhere near Waterford or Cork. Westwards it went from Dublin, across the great Central Plain by Athlone, Ballinasloe and Athenry to Galway City. Travelling politicians seemed to abound on the Midland Great Western; on its trains you heard more people talking Gaelic than, it seemed, on all the other Irish railways put together; even about the massive Broadstone terminus in Dublin (in these days a lorry depot) there was a breath from remote Aran. Going west, you could see a spanking American girl dressed up to the nines, step off the train into the arms of a shawled and barefoot Biddy who was probably her elder sister who had stayed at home. One of Synge's finest pieces of descriptive writing involves a wild journey on a Midland Great Western night train from Galway to Dublin.*

Beyond Galway, the main line continued as a light railway to Clifden under the Twelve Bens and along the north shore of Galway Bay. It was a spectacular run and carried an important tourist traffic in the summer, though it was never a gold-mine

* In *The Aran Islands.*

to the company. Galway being a terminus, the farther west trains used to back out of it and make a fresh start at the junction outside. Like so many Irish light railways, originally constructed with Government or Baronial assistance, it fell on evil days; to-day its place knows it no more, the mountains of Connemara resound not the echo of a locomotive whistle, and the stations sadly serve the purpose of handling consignments for the motor vans and lorries of Coras Iompair Eireann. Yet once, the arrival of the Mail was Clifden's principal spectacle, and what a jaundiced Englishman might dismiss simply as an old 2–4–0 engine with a high-sounding name, clanking in with four or five miscellaneous carriages, was in very truth the Connemara Express.

The main line from Dublin to Mullingar was the M.G.W.R. show section. The best train made the $50\frac{1}{4}$ miles run non-stop in 72 minutes. Dublin to Galway, $126\frac{1}{2}$ miles, was covered in 3 hours 10 minutes. These were not startling times, but the company's permanent way sometimes caused anything in the nature of fast running to have physiological disadvantages. A number of very long branches diverged northwards from the main line. First came the Meath line to Kingscourt, 43 miles from Clonsilla Junction and 50 from Dublin. The Sligo line from Mullingar was in truth a second main line, carrying important traffic to Sligo via Longford, and it still maintains that status. The Mayo lines, diverging at Athlone, originally formed the Great Northern and Western Railway, which the M.G.W.R. absorbed, and served a wide area of wild Connacht country, extending to Westport and, eventually to Achill Island. The Westport and Achill line, of delectable remoteness, has now gone the way of the Clifden line.

Midland Great Western trains were always distinctive, quaint and antique as many of them were once one got away from the crack services. Martin Atock's little locomotives with their floridly curved cabs, wildly varying names and showy finish, carrying their headlamps between the buffers, were like nothing else in Ireland, or, for that matter, in Great Britain. Features of the Great Southern and Western trains might remind you remotely of Crewe; those of the Great Northern Railway of Ireland were made deliberately to resemble, in many respects, the trains of the English Great Northern, but the Midland Great Western trains were entirely distinctive. There was a whimsical variety about their names; that there should be an *Emerald Isle* and a *Celtic* and a *Faugh a Ballagh* was scarcely unexpected, but Mr. Atock, one of the gentlest and most courteous of locomotive superintendents, saw to it that while he might build a *Hibernia*, there were also *Britannia*, *Caledonia* and *Cambria*. The *Empress of Austria* expressed Irish admiration for a royal lady of sound sporting reputation; three odd little tank engines with single driving wheels, more pretty than useful, were appropriately called *Bee*, *Elf* and *Fairy*; as you loafed northwards from Manulla Junction to Killala, behind *Swift* or *Racer*, you could reflect that some of the names were less suitable, but nobody minded much.

Edward Cusack's engines, built during the present century, were much more imposing, and for a few years in the early nineteen hundreds were glorified by a royal blue livery, with blue and white carriages to match. Blue is, however, a notoriously bad wearing colour, and evidently the great Atlantic gales roaring up Galway Bay were too much for it, on the Midland Great Western, for a return was soon made to Atock's emerald green, with brown for the carriages. Like all the Irish main-line railways, the Midland Great Western was of 5 ft. 3 in. gauge, giving the engines a slightly squat appearance when viewed head-on, though this was nothing like the elephantine forward aspect of a 7 ft. gauge train on the Great Western.

The best carriage stock of the Midland Great Western was excellent, apart from a denial of third-class access to restaurant cars. For a royal visit in 1910 Mr. Cusack built a most superb saloon carriage, the main compartment of which was made like a miniature pillared hall of surpassing elegance, while the ends were curved and panelled, with large observation windows. The ordinary carriages were very ordinary, and in lighting the carriage department showed a touching attachment to the old oil-pot lamp, dropped through a hole in the roof some time after sundown. But in this repect the Midland Great Western was scarcely isolated among Irish railways; it must also be borne in mind that it was by no means a wealthy undertaking, and that when it could afford to spread itself it did handsomely.

To this day, there is an extraordinary atmosphere about the Kingsbridge terminus in Dublin, which was the headquarters of the old Great Southern and Western. There it stands, with its great block of offices executed in the most elegant Victorian imitation of Inigo Jones, giving a façade that prepares you for a vast terminus. Yet behind that brave front lies a quiet little station with only two platforms under a cavernous roof. There is a sense of anticlimax about one on first entering the classic portals of Kingsbridge, comparable, farther abroad, to that produced by Helsingfors with its superb station building backing on to a bleak array of completely uncovered platforms. But then, there were no vast stations in Dublin as in the cities of England and Scotland; one sought in vain for the peers of Waterloo, Waverley, St. Enoch, or Perth General. Westland Row on the Dublin and South Eastern and Amiens Street on the Great Northern provided the nearest approaches to anything like a large station. But architecturally the Dublin stations made a brave show; there was nothing in London like Kingsbridge, just described, or the Palladian front of Amiens Street. On the Great Southern and Western, the company's flare for showy architecture cropped up again in the works and running shed at Inchicore, which were as grandly academic as the buildings of a locomotive department could be. Inchicore at least rivalled the face which Balliol presents to the Broad at Oxford, and was rather better than Keble. Inchicore produced some famous men, too. Thence, to England, came Ivatt to the Great Northern, McDonnell to the North Eastern, Aspinall to the Lancashire and Yorkshire, and Maunsell to the South Eastern and Chatham and, subsequently, the Southern.

But McDonnell, before going to Inchicore, had been under Webb at Crewe, and there was a peculiarly London and North Western flavour about many of the Great Southern and Western locomotives in consequence. There was, however, little of the

North Western about other features of the railway, at any rate in its earlier days. Back in the 'forties, it had been laid with iron bridge rails which were all right in their way and capable of sustaining the little Sharp and Bury engines of those days, and Wakefield's scarcely robust types which succeeded them. But thirty years on, the old rails were still there, and on them the Great Southern and Western optimistically endeavoured to provide a train service as of yore. Two things could break, and often did. One was an engine spring; in McDonnell's time spare springs were always carried on the locomotives so that the enginemen could give first aid whenever something happened. The other probable breakage was that of a rail. Of course, there ought to have been a succession of frightful derailments, yet nothing unduly awful happened through this cause. The one really bad smash on the Great Southern and Western in its early days, that at Straffan in 1853, was a rear collision. When a rail broke, its useful life was not ended. The broken pieces were carefully trimmed and usefully employed in filling some gap on a branch line which had gone from bad to worse. The motion and rail-joint noises of a Great Southern and Western local train in the early 'seventies were fantastic.

By degrees, the old rails were weeded out and the company adopted quite a respectable permanent way with bullhead rails in chairs. The Midland Great Western, by the way, used flat-bottom rails as on American and Continental railways. The Great Southern and Western Railway grew into the largest Irish system, with some 1,121¾ miles of route, all broad gauge, compared with 561 miles on the Great Northern and 538 miles on the Midland Great Western. Its route mileage had been considerably swelled by taking in the Waterford, Limerick and Western Railway, an entirely provincial line extending from Waterford to Limerick, with certain branches, including a long one to Tralee and a very long one, forming a prolongation of the main line after reversal at Limerick, to Collooney Junction by Sligo. The Waterford, Limerick and Western also made a valuable contribution to the English Railway world, in the person of J. G. Robinson, who became locomotive superintendent of the Great Central Railway. His locomotives for the Irish line bore little resemblance to those with which he became famous at Gorton Works, but there was a marked suggestion of Great Western practice about them, particularly so in the case of the 2–4–0 express engines with their large brass domes. Not even the Waterford red livery could destroy that Swindonian aspect.

As remarked, McDonnell had given the Great Southern and Western engines proper a distinctly Crewe flavour. They were black, lined out vermilion and white; there was the same oblong panel-plate below the cab side-sheets, which last, however, were more generous than on the skimpy North-Western article. The cast number-plates were almost pure Crewe, though the archaic London and North Western timber-framed tender was not perpetuated in Ireland. Succeeding chiefs at Inchicore never quite got rid of the Creweisms, though there was little of the North Western about Robert Coey's 321 class express engines of 1907. These were notable for, among other things, their tapered boilers, at that time little used except, in England, by the Great Western Railway under G. J. Churchward, whose engines were otherwise quite unlike those of Inchicore. They were built for a short life only, Mr. Coey having got the idea, probably from bitter experience with the wide variety of antiques left by his predecessors, that the ideal locomotive's life should be short and gay. That may have been the intention, but the 321 class, albeit much rebuilt, is still doing useful work for Coras Iompair Eireann.

The Great Southern and Western, by virtue of its branch to Valentia Harbour, possessed what is still the most westerly railway station in Europe, indeed, quite a considerable mileage of the company's system was nearer to America than anything in Portugal. The main line, served by some of the best trains in Ireland, was that from Dublin to Cork, running south west to Charleville and thence south. Then there was an entirely separate main line running from Rosslare Harbour to Killarney and beyond, latterly carrying a very considerable tourist traffic from England via Fishguard, intersecting the Dublin-Cork line at Mallow. Limerick Junction, where the main line crossed the old Waterford, Limerick and Western, possessed—and still possesses—what is probably the most extraordinary railway station in Europe. Beside it the inverted delta of Inverness, the Ashchurch triangle, and the three-gauge stations of Sweden and Southern France are simple and commonplace. The two lines cross on the level, and both the main-line and the Waterford and Limerick trains have to perform a complicated acrobatic feat, a series of backings and other manœuvres, before they can get alongside a platform. Limerick Junction is, indeed the most Irish station imaginable, for every train must go past it, or through it, before it can get into it at all.*

Before the 1914–18 war, the Great Southern and Western possessed the fastest train in Ireland, a combined Cork and Killarney express, which ran from Kingsbridge to Mallow at an average speed of 50 m.p.h. with a locomotive stop at Bally-brophy. The usual load out of Dublin consisted of two bogie coaches and a van for Cork, the same for Killarney, and two bogie coaches for Ennis which were slipped at Limerick Junction. The main line, though not mountainous in the Pennine or Scottish sense of the word, was far from easy. At the Dublin end there was a sharp climb to Inchicore and a fairly continuous rise for thirty miles to Kildare. From Glanmire Road, Cork, there was a more difficult start than from Dublin, including two miles at 1 in 60. The mails and other heavy trains have always been piloted as far as Blarney, and for many years this notable bank had been the scene of such prodigies as triple-headed expresses, the pilot engine being added even if there are two engines on already. An excellent run was made by a viceregal special early in the present century, with one of Coey's older 4-4-0 engines, No. 301, *Victoria*, built in 1900. Dublin to Mallow was covered at an average of 58 m.p.h., allowing for a four-minute water stop at Thurles, and from Mallow to Killarney, $40\frac{3}{4}$ miles over single track throughout, the average speed was just under 50 m.p.h. This was most creditable, even allowing for the light load of three bogie vehicles.

* Brilliant exposition in the *Railway Magazine* for May 1939.

In the viceregal saloon, originally built for a royal visit in 1903, the Great Southern and Western exemplified its occasional indulgence in gorgeous decoration. There was an *art-nouveau* reception room and a baroque ante-room of surpassing splendour. The Dublin furnishing house of Sibthorpe possessed an artist particularly gifted in the matter of painted ceilings; his services were several times in demand by the Great Southern and Western Railway, and so gorgeous were the results achieved, not only in the saloon carriage mentioned, but in several dining cars built about the turn of the century, that they were carefully recorded by the expedient of placing the G.S. and W. official camera on its back, with the lens pointing straight upwards at the Arcadian splendours overhead. Not even the Manchester, Sheffield and Lincolnshire Railway, which knew a good deal about this sort of thing, could touch the Great Southern and Western when it came to dining-car ceilings.

Surrounded by the Great Southern and Western on its landward sides was the Cork, Bandon and South Coast Railway. It was a small railway, although of broad gauge, with only 93¾ miles of route, but its character was strongly developed. In its earliest form, it extended from Ballinhassig to Bandon, passengers being conveyed in and out of Cork by coach until the completion of a peculiarly steep and foul tunnel, and traffic was moved in those days by W. Bridges Adams' patent light locomotives. These, however, came before our time. In those same far-off days, the Cork and Bandon Railway, as it then was, distinguished its engines by glorious Gaelic names, which were moreover inscribed on the plates in Erse, and not Latin characters. In later years the C.B. and S.C. locomotives were, with two noteworthy exceptions, of quite orthodox tank-engine types, culminating in some handsome 4–6–0 tanks, a form seldom seen in Great Britain but which did good work anywhere between Cork and Bantry Bay. The exceptions were American. Now several British railways had invested in American locomotives as a stopgap about the turn of the century, when British builders were so full with orders that they could take no more. But most of these were to a greater or lesser extent anglicized, usually in the design of the boilers. Cork, Bandon and South Coast Nos. 19 and 20, on the contrary, were as rank a pair of Yankee goats as ever came out of the Baldwin Locomotive Works. The only un-American things about them were the European-type buffers and drawgear, and the smokebox doors. They were 0–6–2 saddle-tanks with outside cylinders having the valves on top. Even the chimneys and dome casings were of the characteristic Baldwin type. They appeared in 1900 and did useful work during the locomotive shortage, though their life was brief. No. 20 was scrapped in 1912 and No. 19 lasted two years longer. In the meantime, new 4–6–0 tanks were built with the same numbers; both the nineteens could be seen arriving at Cork on successive trains.

The C.B. and S.C.R. main line ran from Cork to Drimoleague Junction, whence one branch went down to Skibbereen and Baltimore and a shorter one to Bantry. Both branches had interesting connections. From Bantry the company ran a full-blooded service of four-horse coaches over the Prince of Wales' Route through Glengarriff and Kenmare to Killarney; the 3 ft. gauge Schull and Skibbereen Light Railway pursued a gloriously meandering course round Roaring Water Bay. Nearer Cork there were the Kinsale, Clonakilty, and Timoleague and Courtmacsherry lines. The Cork, Bandon and South Coast, whether in its independent days or under the successive regimes of the Great Southern Railways and the C.I.E., has ever been a fascinating line. May its oft-threatened sacrifice to the Great God Motor be indefinitely delayed!

Going back to Dublin, let us next consider the Dublin, Wicklow and Wexford Railway, or, as it became at the beginning of 1907, the Dublin and South Eastern. With but 160 miles of route, this might have been regarded as a lesser railway, but it was indeed an important main line. Two particular sources of passenger traffic were the elegant suburbs which grew up around Dublin Bay and Dalkey Bay, and the beautiful country of the Wicklow mountains. It had two distinct lines out of Dublin, whereof the older incorporated the Dublin and Kingstown Railway, the oldest line in Ireland, dating from 1834.

South of Kingstown, as it then was, this line made a spectacular passage round the coast by Killiney. Coastal erosion has caused trouble, necessitating extensive realignments, indeed, it has been one of the most expensive sections of railway in Ireland. The terminus of this line was at Westland Row, whence, in 1891, the City of Dublin Junction Railway was extended across the Liffey to link up with the Great Northern at Amiens Street, with an intermediate station at Tara Street. From Kingstown, in connection with the steamers from England, through carriages were run to distant destinations on the Great Southern and Western, Midland Great Western and Great Northern Railways.

The second D.S.E. line out of Dublin started in a modest way at Harcourt Street, pursuing an inland course to Bray. This was originally the route of the expresses to the south, the best of which was the day mail, consisting of vehicles for Wexford and Waterford, dividing at Macmine, where the Waterford section reversed. It was a nice train, without doing anything startling; its brightest performance was a non-stop run of $14\frac{1}{2}$ miles from New Ross to Waterford.

As on the Great Southern and Western, the trains were of sober aspect and sombre colouring; fine red and gold lines added a subdued note of splendour to the black locomotives; the carriages, scarcely brighter than the G.S. and W's "purple-brown," were dark red with, again, a streak of gold. Some of the express engines had names, usually beginning with either Glen or Rath. No. 68, *Rathcoole* was fated to come to a sad end during the Trouble, in 1923.

From 1897, the Mail was arranged to start from Westland Row, and in 1904 it acquired restaurant car facilities. These at first took a form favoured by the London and South Western at that time, having central corridor coaches served by a kitchen in the van. The train then ran to Waterford at an average speed of just over 31 m.p.h., with seven stops, which included a call at Kingstown Pier entailing two reversals. Third-class passengers, and Wexford people, were excluded from the restaurant cars, which ran to Waterford.

In the older days, the Dublin, Wicklow and Wexford Railway

was distinguished by an incredible collection of ancient loco-motives. There were veterans of the Dublin and Kingstown, there were rakish little 2–4–0 express engines, all elegance and hot air, and there were on the local trains some quite fantastic single tank engines, with long trough-shaped tanks, very tall bellmouthed chimneys, bottle-topped domes, and the enginemen accommodated in something between a hansom cab and an enormous tin box.

Of much more Anglo-Irish character was the Great Northern Railway, which, as remarked, obviously set out to copy in certain details the peculiarities of its English namesake. The livery was nearly the same; the more modern carriages, especially the dining-car stock, had an extraordinarily Don-castrian flavour about them.

The Great Northern Railway of Ireland, with its main line of 112¾ miles from Amiens Street, Dublin, through Drogheda and Dundalk to Belfast, was formed as late as 1876 by amalga-mation. In the previous year there had been a fusion of the Dublin and Drogheda Railway and the Dublin and Belfast Junction Railway, to form the Northern of Ireland Railway. The second amalgamation, which produced the G.N.R. (I), included the Ulster Railway, one of the oldest lines in Ireland, the first section of which was opened in 1839. By means of a number of very long branches, the Great Northern reached Bundoran in the west and Derry in the north, and as part owner, with the Belfast and Northern Counties, of the 3 ft. gauge County Donegal Railways, it had access to the remote termini of Glenties and Killybegs. At Dundalk and Newry it connected with the quaint little Dundalk, Newry and Greenore Railway, owned by the London and North Western and forming, in its equipment, a remarkable miniature of the great English company, worked by six old Ramsbottom saddle-tank engines, a dozen six-wheel carriages of typical Wolverton design, and a couple of hundred goods vehicles in the familiar North Western lead colour.

The Dublin–Belfast expresses were very smart trains indeed, equalled in Ireland only by the best Great Southern and

Western trains between Dublin and Cork. In one respect the carriages were superior to those of any other long-distance railway in the British Isles, for the company went straight from the primeval oil-pot lamp to Stone's electric lighting, with generators on the bogies, taking this up universally when most railways were tinkering about with gas mantles and their complementary abominations. The restaurant car service was of high degree, though the cars were floridly, solidly Philistine in the style of their decoration, and attained not the picturesque magnificence of those on the Great Southern and Western. As far back as 1895, when Ireland generally was a land of glumly non-corridor compartments and refreshment room dyspepsia, what was officially described as a "breakfast carriage" was put on the boat trains between Kingstown Pier and Belfast, working through from Westland Row to Amiens Street, of course, by the City of Dublin Junction line. It consisted of a side-corridor eight-wheeler with two first-class, two second-class and a kitchen compartment, together with lavatories and a luggage locker. The meals—breakfast going north and late luncheon coming south—were served on movable oblong tables set up in the compartments, forerunners of the folding peg-legged tables employed for compartment service of meals later on. During the present century the Great Northern adopted the conventional type of dining car, using, at first, twelve-wheelers with clerestory roofs, strongly resembling those on the contemporary Flying Scotsman. The fastest run on the G.N.R. (I) in 1909 was that of the up evening express, which ran from Drogeda to Dublin at 48.85 m.p.h. start-to-stop.

The older locomotives were of 2–4–0 and 0–4–2 types, more dainty than powerful, but the end of the last century saw the introduction of a number of handsome 4–4–0 bogie engines. The forerunners of these were two bogie singles with inside cylinders, the first of their kind, named *Victoria* and *Albert*, and built by Beyer, Peacock and Company in 1885. The heavier dining-car trains were beyond their powers of timekeeping; they were converted to small-wheeled 4–4–0's for branch line service.

Survivor of the Salisbury Smash: Drummond 4–4–0 No. 421, London and South Western Railway, hauling an up Ilfracombe express, between Raynes Park and Wimbledon

*[F. Moore's Railway Photographs]*

When Liners called at Fishguard: American boat express hauled by a "City" and a "Bulldog," leaving for Paddington, Great Western Railway

*[F. Moore's Railway Photographs]*

Broad-gauge Days: Above is a local train at Cornwood, Great Western Railway, with one of the 10 ft. 6 in. wide coaches of 1877 at the rear; beyond is the old Brunel viaduct with timber arches. Below: One of the later eight-foot singles is passing Bourton with an up express, on mixed-gauge track

[*Locomotive and General Railway Photographs*]

Badminton on up South Wales express passing over Goring troughs, Great Western Railway
[*T. F. Budden*]

Southbound train near Savernake, Midland and South Western Junction Railway,
hauled by 4-4-4 tank engine No. 18
[*Locomotive and General Railway Photographs*]

S. W. Johnson's small-wheeled 4-4-0 type for the Somerset and Dorset Joint Railway
[*Locomotive and General Railway Photographs*]

Paddington–Bristol Express, Great Western Railway, hauled by G. J. Churchward's unique Pacific engine, No. 111, *The Great Bear*. This photograph was taken since 1914 but is included as one of the few showing this once famous engine in motion

[*F. Moore's Railway Photographs*]

A characteristic Great Central express of the nineteen-hundreds, hauled by
Robinson 4–4–0 locomotive No. 1040 and including some of the carriages specially
built for the London extension in the late 'nineties
[*F. Moore's Railway Photographs*]

Goods train at Manchester, London Road, Great Central Railway; Sacré goods
No. 471 piloted by saddle tank No. 275 B
[*W. H. Whitworth*]

Train from Towcester at Stratford-on-Avon, East and West Junction Railway, April 20, 1897; Beyer Peacock 2–4–0 tank engine
[*George Dow Collection*]

Haverhill-Chappel train, Colne Valley and Halstead Railway, passing Colne Valley Junction Box, July 29, 1911; 2–4–2 tank No. 3
[*K. A. C. R. Nunn*]

North Eastern royal train (Great Northern saloon fourth from tender) hauled
by Wilson Worsdell's 4–6–0 No. 2010

*[L.N.E.R. Records]*

London and North Western royal train, headed by Lancashire, Derbyshire and
East Coast 0–6–2 tank engine No. 26, carrying King Edward VII to Doncaster races,
September 1906

*[L.N.E.R. Records]*

Matthew Stirling's
press engine No.
Hull and Barn
Railway

[*F. Moore's Railway
Photographs*]

Down West of Engl
express approach
Winchfield, Lon
and South Wes
Railway, in 18
Adams' seven-fo
No. 594

[*T. F. Budden*]

One of Aspinall's F
flyers in action, I
cashire and Yorks
Railway, about
years ago

[*F. Moore's Railwa
Photographs*]

On June 12, 1889, there occurred on the Great Northern Railway of Ireland a very terrible accident, recorded here on account of the important results which it had thereafter on all railways in Great Britain and Ireland. A fifteen-coach excursion train, hauled by the old 2-4-0 engine No. 86 and fitted with Smith's non-automatic vacuum brake, started out from Armagh to Warrenpoint. There were incidents at the start. The driver complained to the Armagh stationmaster that the train was beyond the power of his engine on the three-mile climb, most of it at 1 in 75, which began about a quarter of a mile east of Armagh. The stationmaster, out of temper that day for some reason, pooh-poohed the driver's argument that a better description of the train should have been sent to the Dundalk shed, so that a more powerful locomotive could have been provided for this special working. Other drivers, he said, were less fussy. Someone brightly suggested that the excursion should wait for the very lightly-loaded ordinary train to come up and bank it in the rear, but the excursion driver, now in a great rage with the stationmaster, said that as they had thought fit to put him on his mettle, why, sure, he would show them, so he would! Near the summit, No. 86 stalled, and a council of war was held with an acting inspector who was travelling on the train. This man decided to divide the train and take the two parts, in turn, to Hamilton's Bawn, the next station. Such a plan, reasonable to-day, was extremely rash on this steep gradient with a train fitted with a non-automatic brake, which became inoperative in the detached vehicles once the hose was disconnected. Stones were placed under the wheels of two vehicles in the uncoupled section, and it was supposed (!) that the hand-brake was on in the brake composite carriage at the rear. It was then found that No. 86 had stopped on dead-centre and she had to be backed slightly before she could start with the front section of the divided train. This operation pushed the ten detached carriages over the stones, and they began to run back. Passengers had overflowed into the guard's compartment, and two excited people, trying to help the guard with the hand-brake, the only brake now in operation, appear to have turned it the wrong way.

Whatever happened, the results were disastrous. About 1½ miles down the hill, on top of a 50 ft. embankment, the ten runaway vehicles, now running at great speed, pitched into the following ordinary train. The engine of this, a small 0-4-2, was thrown over on its side, but the destruction of the colliding carriages was terrific. The last three vehicles were smashed to splinters, killing eighty people and injuring 260. Of the ordinary train, five out of the six vehicles now began to run back in their turn. The guard managed to stop them, but they were nearly struck by the tender and the leading vehicle, a horsebox, which came down after them. Fortunately the driver of the ordinary train kept his head and provided an example of courageous coolness in the midst of the otherwise disgraceful circumstances. After the impact which had sent his engine over, he remained on the underailed tender and succeeded in stopping this and the horsebox by his handbrake just before they would have struck his own train.

For some years, agitation had been growing over the question of continuous brakes. This dreadful smash condemned all passenger train brakes that were not automatic in action, and automatic continuous power brakes were made compulsory for all passenger trains, by the Regulation of Railways Act, 1889.

Of the many delightful stations in the Irish provinces, Sligo took a lot of beating, and still does so. Its gaunt barns were at the end of that long second-string main line of the Midland Great Western from Mullingar, but a little way south of it was Collooney Junction. To the untutored, this could be merely just the lonely spot that W. B. Yeats had properly chosen for the home of a reed whispering about the weary of heart, but the railway amateur instantly thought of it, and the line into Sligo, as an omnium gatherum of otherwise widely separated railways. The Waterford, Limerick and Western, and, later, the Great Southern and Western as its successor, came meandering in from Claremorris. Then into it from eastwards came the Sligo, Leitrim and Northern Counties Railway, to-day the sole survivor of Ireland's minor broad-gauge lines, coming down from Enniskillen with a main line 49 miles long and no branches.

98

The Leitrim company opened its railway in 1882, and since then has maintained a sturdy individualism through all the ups and downs of Irish railway history. Its original locomotives, which still provide the backbone of its motive power, though larger engines have been built in more recent years, were a class of 0-6-4 tank designed and built by Beyer, Peacock and Company. This type of 0-6-4 tank engine was then unknown in England, though, also in Ireland, the Great Southern and Western sampled it. One of the Leitrim engines, *Hazlewood*, was deliberately derailed on Glenfarne Bank during the Trouble and rolled down the steeply sloped embankment. She was, however, luckier than the Dublin and South Eastern's *Rathcoole*, and is still running at the time of writing. Several carriages were, however, less fortunate. The Irish Government compensated the railway, which replaced the casualties in 1925 with some remarkable tricomposite bogie vehicles. These come outside the strict limits of our period, but deserve reference. For one thing, they were the first clerestory vehicles owned by the Sligo, Leitrim and Northern Counties and at the same time the last to be built for any steam railway in the British Isles. Secondly, they came at a time when first-class traffic was declining through private motor competition, so they were economically equipped with only one first-class compartment each, and that divided by a longitudinal partition with a sliding door, to accommodate both smokers and non-smokers without mutual offence. This arrangement of subdivision harked back to days long before our period, for the Great Western in England and the Midland Great Western in Ireland both employed it in the eighteen-forties.

There was little competition between Irish railways. To an even greater extent than the Scottish lines, they kept to their own territories where their monopolies were unbroken until petrol challenged steam in earnest. Between Belfast (Queen's Quay) and Newcastle, the Belfast and County Down Railway ran a service more or less competitive with that of the Great Northern from Belfast (Great Victoria Street) and the same place, but the last section of the Great Northern run had to be made over the B. and C.D. Castlewellan branch. In the other direction, the Great Northern ran from Belfast to Derry on a somewhat circuitous course through Portadown, Omagh and Strabane, while the Belfast and Northern Counties pursued a northerly course via Coleraine and thence along the coast and the shores of Lough Foyle. Neither line from Belfast to Derry produced any really startling trains; the Northern Counties trains, though taking a shorter route, had to reverse at Greenisland after beginning the journey on the Larne line, running north-east. From Belfast, Derry lay west-by-north. The express engine would come on at Greenisland, the first part of the journey being made behind any sort of a locomotive, such as an undersized Beyer Peacock 2–4–0 tank.

All this sounds rather woebegone, which was not the case. The Northern Counties was in many ways a smart little railway, and served its corner of Ulster well. Moreover, it penetrated a considerable stretch of wild country which might have remained untouched by railway transport, by means of a narrow-gauge system of its own. Out of its 219 miles of route, more than sixty miles were on the 3 ft. gauge, including the Ballymena and Larne line, over which a service of narrow-gauge boat trains enabled passengers to Derry via the Stranraer route to bypass Belfast, picking up the main broad-gauge line at a point where it was well on its way westwards. At a later date, after the close of our period, the narrow-gauge Ballycastle Railway was also taken in. To-day, alas, this is the only Northern Counties narrow-gauge line to retain a passenger service, and in Ballycastle it now possesses the nearest railway station to Port Ellen, Campbeltown, and other places in Western Scotland!

The Northern Counties was one of those lines that introduced to railway history an outstanding personality. This was Bowman Malcolm, who became its locomotive engineer in 1876, at the age of 22. He was a believer in compound locomotives, using the Worsdell–von Borries two-cylinder system, which gave them a characteristic slow exhaust of two beats only per revolution. Two 7 ft. 4–4–0's, *Jubilee* and *Parkmount*, built in 1895, were for long the stars of the Northern Counties. On the narrow-gauge lines, Malcolm used 2–4–2 compound tank engines with outside cylinders and gear.

The Belfast and Northern Counties Railway assumed that title in 1860 and was made up of various lines amalgamated to form a whole. One of the quaintest of its later constituents was the Portstewart line, a 3 ft. gauge steam tramway pure and simple with the same sort of "dummy" locomotives, all-enclosed, as one once saw on numerous street tramways in the Midlands and North of England, hauling, in that rather remote place, the most towny-looking double-deck tramcars with a few odd vans thrown in for luggage and freight. It was taken over by the Northern Counties in 1897. Though its place knows it no more, two steam dummies were preserved. One is still stored at Belfast at the time of writing; the other was acquired by the Hull Museum and, there, together with the even more ancient tramcar off Ryde Pier, Isle of Wight, which had been lovingly restored, it came to a sad end in one of the air raids of 1941.

The Midland Railway acquired the Northern Counties by amalgamation in 1903, but it continued, under the Northern Counties Committee, as an autonomous railway, and at the end of our period the venerable Mr. Malcolm (he was still only 60) remained at the head of its locomotive department.

Most imposing of Ireland's numerous narrow-gauge railways was the County Donegal, with headquarters at Stranorlar, which, as already remarked, was a joint undertaking of the Northern Counties and the Great Northern. These connected with it at Strabane and (Great Northern only) at Ballyshannon. It had 91¼ miles of route at the end of our period, and its best trains, which included quite comfortable lavatory-fitted stock and observation cars, possessed much more of the main-line atmosphere than other Irish narrow-gauge railways, even though winter warmth continued to be provided by the unassuming hot-water tin. In 1912, three 2–6–4 tank engines were acquired for non-stop running between Derry and Donegal, 46 miles, which distance was covered at 35 m.p.h. start to stop. The Donegal's status as a joint railway dated from 1906. In recent years, with Irish minor railways falling on very evil days, the company has shown good fighting spirit, indeed, it was the first railway in the British Isles to recapture lost traffic with diesel railcars.

The Belfast and County Down Railway, of 5 ft. 3 in. gauge, to which I have already referred, was of some antiquity, most of it having been opened between 1848 and 1859, when it reached Downpatrick, later the junction for Ardglass and Newcastle. While it carried a fair agricultural traffic, like other railways, it was an important holiday line from quite an early date, serving various seaside places of which Bangor was reached in 1865. This, however, was carried out by a separate company, which took over the existing line between Ballymacarret Junction, Belfast, and Holywood, and was not merged finally into the B. and C.D. until 1884.

Although primarily a local railway, the Belfast and County Down worked a distinctly creditable service of its kind, chiefly with tank engines. At one time, observing the next-door example of Bowman Malcolm on the Northern Counties, it placed several two-cylinder compound engines in service, though these did not enjoy the success and the long careers of those on the neighbour railway. In 1897, for a visit of the Duke and Duchess of York (later George V and Queen Mary), the company produced an extremely elegant royal train. Hauled by 2-4-0 locomotive No. 24, one of the compounds, it consisted of two vans and two family saloons, all six-wheeled, a bogie coach and an extremely handsome bogie saloon with a clerestory roof.

With the Belfast and County Down Railway and its compact system of 80 route miles, we must leave the Irish railways for the present. Some of the most interesting lines in Ireland come rather under the category of minor railways, and, in at least one case, that of oddities.

# CHAPTER SIX

# LOCOMOTIVES

## *Historical Sketch*

IF we could flash ourselves back into the year 1874, while remaining fully aware of things that have happened since then, we would be surprised less by the archaic design of many locomotives than by their enormous variety. We would find the ancient side by side with the relatively familiar, moreover, we would be astonished at the variations between the practice of different companies in different parts of Great Britain and Ireland. Something of this has been suggested in the Irish chapter just past; even in the present century, while there were fine modern locomotives on the Great Southern and Western main line, there were elsewhere engines that took you back to the dawn of locomotive history.

In 1874 the best trains in the South of England, which were those of the Great Western and the London and South Western, were being worked by locomotives of extremely antiquated type, even though they might be newly built, and this was the more remarkable in that the two railways mentioned were utterly different in practice. As we have seen, for its broad-gauge lines the Great Western clung tenaciously to the ancient Iron Duke class 4–2–2 eight-footers, originally designed by Daniel Gooch, and built new ones when the veterans wore out, right up to 1888. Perhaps the broad-gauge engines afford an unfair example, with the shadow of abolition hanging over them for so many years, but at that time many Great Western locomotives, broad and standard gauge alike, had the same sandwich frames, built up of wooden planking bolted between iron plates, as the first engines the company had ever possessed. William Dean's very handsome seven-foot singles of 1878–79 had oak sandwich frames of exactly the same type as Stephenson's *North Star* and *Morning Star*, built for the G.W.R. in 1837. One reason for the continuation of such old-fashioned practice on the Great Western was that the sandwich frames were elastic, and therefore took kindly to the very rigid "baulk road" —bridge rails on heavy longitudinal sleepers with cross transoms —which formed the Great Western's standard permanent way throughout the Victorian era.

On the South Western, as remarked, the standard locomotives were old-fashioned in quite another way. Except for some Beyer Peacock goods engines and a number of extreme veterans, South Western engines in 1874 generally combined outside cylinders with inside frames. Joseph and George Beattie, father and son, had been successively in command at Nine Elms Works since 1850, and although both were extremely clever and ingenious engineers, there were strong signs of that stagnation which can come over a family business in the course of long years. Until 1875, when some Metropolitan-type 4–4–0 tanks were ordered outside for the new Plymouth road, there was not a bogie engine on the L.S.W.R., nor, indeed, an eightwheeler of any kind. From 1859 to 1876, the standard express engine was a 2–4–0 with its cylinders in front of the leading wheels, a small low-pitched boiler with a large dome over the firebox, which already had a raised steam space over it, an immensely tall, slender chimney, and coupled wheels of 6 ft. 6 in. or 7 ft. diameter. Latterly they had copper chimney caps and beautifully curved bright brass casings to dome and safety-valves, but they certainly looked very light and faery for a railway with such undulating main lines as the London and South Western.

But what the Beatties' 2–4–0 express engines lacked in modernity of general design, they made up in accessories. They were as richly endowed with clever gadgets as French engines; they had been the first in England to burn coal instead of coke on a large scale, for which reason, perhaps, the London and South Western was always known to Great Western men at Basingstoke as "Blaze-an'-smoke." Joseph Beattie had devised various formidably complicated boilers to ensure complete combustion of such dirty, common fuel, and to prevent such reproaches as the Great Western one just mentioned. In its final form the Beattie boiler had a double firebox, fed by two firedoors. The inner firebox was supposed to be kept in a highly incandescent state, in order to burn the sooty products of the heavier firing carried on in the rearmost box. Various complicated forms of feedwater heaters, with donkey pumps instead of injectors, went with the coal-burning boiler, the engine was externally finished in chocolate with elaborate lining-out, and given a high-sounding name like *Ganymede*, or *Circe*, or *Sultana*, and everyone admired. McConnell on the North Western and Cudworth on the South Eastern, had likewise devised variously complicated boilers in the cause of Coal without Tears, until somebody discovered that as far back as 1859 Matthew Kirtley on the Midland had been using a generous firebox with a brick arch, which could burn coal efficiently without any need for such complications as the water-bridges, midfeathers, combustion chambers, perforated firebricks and all the rest that Joseph Beattie, Cudworth and McConnell had been tinkering with for so long. It should be realized that there was then far less consultation between mechanical engineers than now, the reticence of their respective departments was terrific, the technical press was less informative and less influential, and the engineering profession went on generally in a series of watertight compartments. The Beatties were especially suspicious of anyone knowing anything about their work—true, the old patent laws were full of holes—and an innocent admirer trying to sketch a Beattie engine from the station platform was liable to be hounded from the premises. The later work of George Beattie deserves notice before we leave this redoubtable family. Valves were his heart's delight, as boilers were his father's. He designed the best balanced slide valves of his time, using a very long lap, and in a series of 4–4–0 locomotives, the South-Western's first bogie express engines, built in 1876, he made a brave attempt to employ piston valves. This was unfortunately premature in the light of metallurgical development, and the engines in question failed miserably.

A number of 4–4–0 bogie express engines appeared on various British railways during the 'seventies, anticipating the common practice of years to come. Curiously, several promising-looking designs, such as the Beattie bogies just mentioned, gave very disappointing results. William Adams's "Ironclad" 4–4–0's on the Great Eastern, built in 1876, the forerunners of his much more successful express engines on the London and South Western, saw very little passenger service; they were sluggish on the road and were speedily turned over to main-line goods trains. On the other hand, and at the same time, when Adams completely rebuilt some old Sinclair 2–4–0's with bogies and larger boilers, the results were happy and the engines did well on those duties for which the "Ironclads" had been intended. George Brittain, in 1877, built five 7 ft. 4–4–0 express engines with outside cylinders for the Caledonian Railway. These suffered to a greater extent than most locomotives from the then prevailing defect of insufficient boiler power. Dugald Drummond rebuilt them with larger boilers in the 'eighties, with some improvement.

The one really good design of outside-cylinder 4–4–0 locomotive produced at this time was David Jones's Duke class built for the Highland Railway in 1874. It was an enlarged bogie version of the ancient Crewe 2–4–0 type brought out by Alexander Allan in the late 'forties, much used in its day by the London and North Western and several of the Scottish railways, and its design was based on experience with two such engines to which bogies had been added in 1873, on the Dingwall and Skye line of the Highland Railway. Subject to progressive enlargement, it remained the standard Highland engine for many years.

Standard-gauge 4–4–0 express engines with inside cylinders were remarkably successful from the first. They were more lucky. As we have seen, the first of the characteristic British 4–4–0 type, inside framed and outside cylindered, was North British No. 224, the Tay Bridge engine, together with her twin-sister No. 264 and her younger sisters, the 420 class. James Stirling's magnificent seven-footers for the Glasgow and South Western, built in 1873 and already mentioned, were the first to be used in long-distance main-line service at high speeds, and two 6 ft. 7 in. express engines built for the Great Eastern Railway by S. W. Johnson in 1874 introduced the type to England. It should be mentioned that such engines had had their forerunners on the broad-gauge lines, though with either no bogies or bogies of very primitive type; also that Edward Fletcher had built small-wheeled inside cylinder 4–4–0 engines with double frames for the Whitby line of the North Eastern as far back as 1864.

Johnson took his Great Eastern bogie design to the Midland Railway and, with improvements, built it at Derby from 1876 onwards. The early locomotive history of the London Midland and Scottish Railway was not particularly creditable, but it is interesting to recall that this company of our own time built enlarged Johnson 4–4–0 engines in the nineteen-twenties. They were reliable and fool-proof.

In 1876, also, Dugald Drummond brought to the North British his superb Abbotsford class 4–4–0's, already noticed, providing Scotland, and latterly Southern England, with a prototype that was to last for over 40 years. In 1877, Charles Sacré took up the type on the Manchester, Sheffield and Lincolnshire Railway, in this case using double frames, though the bogies had inside frames only. His engines also were remarkable for their longevity.

On the Great Northern Railway, Patrick Stirling had already, in 1870, produced his *chef-d'oeuvre*, the eight-foot bogie single with outside cylinders, of which the original engine, G.N.R. No. 1, still survives. Perhaps this is one of the most famous classes of locomotive that has ever existed. A South American republic even put a picture of one on a stamp, and when, in 1938, the London and North Eastern fetched No. 1 out of York, put her in working order, collected a train of old six-wheel carriages and ran special excursions with them, the result was an outstanding commercial, as well as sentimental, success. The Great Northern eight-foot single of 1870 and onwards, with its rigidly pivoted bogie, is often regarded as an epitome of Mid-Victorian locomotive practice. Yet, although it was an undoubted favourite with its designer, who would permit no mechanical improvements that might spoil the appearance of the engine, it was in many ways the accident of an accident. It had outside cylinders because, had they been inside, with eight-foot drivers, the low-pitched boiler would not have cleared the crank axle; it had a bogie in spite of Patrick Stirling's dislike of bogies, because that was the only way to support its outside-cylindered front end with the leading dimensions as they were. Finally, its lineage was ancient. The Stirling family were pioneers in mechanical engineering, and in 1839, Stirling's foundry in Dundee built some 2-2-2 passenger locomotives with outside inclined cylinders and inside frames for the Arbroath and Forfar Railway. Eighteen years later the rising generation, in the person of Patrick Stirling, built a much enlarged and improved 2-2-2 express engine for the Glasgow and South Western Railway, in which, however, signs of affinity with the Arbroath and Forfar engine were pronounced. Later examples of the Glasgow and South Western design had the flush-top domeless boiler which came to be regarded as characteristic of Stirling locomotives. It had, among external details, what was to become the typical Stirling muzzle-loader chimney and curved brass safety-valve casing over the firebox. It was this Glasgow and South Western design, again much enlarged and fitted with a bogie, that became the traditional Great Northern express engine from the 'seventies to the 'nineties. It was also copied by John Ramsbottom in his L.N.W.R. Problem class of 1859, though normally this engineer was an inside-cylinder man.

Stirling's bogies were antiquated; they steadied his eight-footers, but can scarcely be credited with providing a flexible wheelbase as the pin was rigid. The modern bogie, with spring-controlled sideplay to the pin, was invented by William Adams and was applied to his 4-4-0 tank engines for the North London Railway during the 'sixties.

The standard goods engine on nearly all English and Irish railways during the 'seventies, and for long after, was the inside cylinder o–6–o, usually with inside frames, though sometimes, particularly on the Great Western, with double or sandwich frames. Early tank engines were often easy adaptations of ordinary passenger and goods types; Adams, as we have seen, and Charles Beyer, used the 4–4–o type for tank engines *before* its general application to tender engines, Scotland, in spite of very hilly main lines, long had an affection for four-coupled goods engines, especially outside-cylinder o–4–2's, a type scarcely used by English railways. Patrick and James Stirling, however, favoured the inside-cylinder o–4–2 mixed-traffic engine, which, during the 'seventies, was developed by S. W. Johnson into the popular o–4–4 bogie tank. Stroudley of the Brighton, who hated bogies, preferred the o–4–2 tank, as exemplified in his admirable D 1 tanks built from 1873 onwards, and Dugald Drummond closely copied these on the North British, soon, however, substituting a four-wheel bogie for the single trailing axle.

The outside-cylinder 2–6–o goods or mixed-traffic locomotive, destined to become exceedingly popular on the home railways in later years, made but a slight showing in the nineteenth century. On the Great Eastern, Adams, with the collaboration of Massey Bromley, produced some interesting but unfortunate goods engines of this type in 1878, and Beyer Peacock built such engines for abroad. The Midland and South Western Junction Railway, bargain-hunting in 1895 and 1897, got two of these; otherwise the British Mogul was unknown in its native country until G. J. Churchward took it up on the Great Western in 1911. Previously there had appeared on the same railway William Dean's "Krugers" and "Aberdares" of 1901–03, though these had double frames and inside cylinders and were not, therefore, true Moguls. There remained a number of outside cylinder 2–6–o's built in America by Baldwin and Schenectady for the Midland, and by the former for the Great Northern and Great Central, during the already-mentioned locomotive shortage of 1899–1900.

Apart from the Great Western, London, Brighton and South Coast, and Great Northern Railways, the express engine with single driving wheels was decidedly on the wane in the eighteen-seventies, though very many were still at work. The London and South Western Railway was the first main-line company to abandon it for good, Joseph Beattie's *Victoria* of 1859 being the last to be built for this company. In 1879, Massey Bromley built some new bogie singles for the Great Eastern Railway, somewhat on the lines of Stirling's famous engines for the Great Northern, with outside cylinders. Stroudley's Brighton engines were of the 2–2–2 type with inside cylinders and inside frames throughout, even on the tenders. They did good work on the Portsmouth road in competition with much more powerful four-coupled engines on the rival South Western. The last 2–2–2 locomotives with *outside* cylinders to be built for a British railway were Sacré's 7 ft. 6 in. express engines of 1882–83 on the Manchester, Sheffield and Lincolnshire Railway. They had marked affinities with the ancient Alexander Allan type, and did good work for some years on the Manchester–Liverpool expresses of the Cheshire Lines.

The longest continuous tradition in locomotive design was, without any doubt, that of the London and North Western Railway. On other lines, styles and peculiarities of design changed as designers retired and new men succeeded them, but on the London and North Western Railway tradition was of surpassing strength. John Ramsbottom, the inventor of the water-trough system, was the founder of that tradition, and every North Western chief mechanical engineer who came after him served it. To many, Ramsbottom is automatically associated with his Problem class 2–2–2 engines with outside cylinders, which in their day were certainly outstanding, but his most important designs were the D X 5 ft. 0–6–0 goods of 1858, and his 6 ft. 7½ in. 2–4–0 express engines of 1866 and onwards. In 1874, Francis Webb produced his 5 ft. 6 in. Precursor and 6 ft. 7½ in. Precedent ("Jumbo") class 2–4–0's which were direct derivatives of the Ramsbottom express engines, as were his "Cauliflower" 5 ft. 0–6–0's, built in 1880, of the Ramsbottom D X. George Whale's Precursor class 4–4–0's of 1904 were much enlarged "Jumbos" with leading bogies; his Experiment class 4–6–o's were a six-coupled variant of this second Precursor class; C. J. Bowen Cooke's George the Fifth class, built from 1910 onwards, was in all essentials a superheated Precursor, and his Prince of Wales 4–6–o's of 1911 and subsequent years were the logical six-coupled variation on the "Georges." As the last "Prince" was built for the London Midland and Scottish, and exhibited at the 1924 Wembley exhibition, we see that the Ramsbottom style of locomotive was perpetuated from what might be termed the Victoria-and-Albert Era to the end of the North Western's separate existence and even after.

But while the style persisted, important innovations took place. F. W. Webb's system of compounding was carried out, in its successive variations, from 1878 onwards. In that year he converted an old engine, and in 1881 built a new one, No. 66, *Experiment*, with two high-pressure cylinders outside and a single large low-pressure cylinder inside. Basically, *Experiment* was a "Jumbo," adapted as indicated, with the important difference that the high-pressure cylinders drove the trailing wheels while the single low-pressure drove the leading, the two driving axles being uncoupled, giving the engine the wheel arrangement 2–2, 2–0 instead of 2–4–0.

The Webb three-cylinder compounds that followed showed important economies in fuel, but equally important wastage in lubricants and repair costs. As already indicated, Webb was an autocratic character who would not brook criticism; the compound locomotive was the delight of his austere life, and he went on building it. The best of the three-cylinder compounds were the Teutonic class of 1889. In 1891 and 1894 came two classes of much larger engines with the 2–2, 2–2 wheel arrangement, outwardly resembling the 2–4–2 then popular in France and Belgium. The first were the Greater Britain class with 7 ft. 1 in. coupled wheels, as in the Teutonics, and the latter the John Hick class, with 6 ft. 3 in. These last were the worst of Webb's three-cylinder compounds, and out of his hearing few had a single good word to say for them. Even the best of the three-cylinder engines had their vagaries; they were often sluggish, and most erratic in the rather important job of getting a train started. It was possible to see one at Euston, hopefully facing the stiff climb to Camden and, beyond it, the long run to the north, but otherwise in the equivocal position of having the rear pair of driving wheels violently slipping in forward gear while the leading (low-pressure) pair solemnly revolved in reverse, owing to non-co-operation on the part of a slip-eccentric gear on the leading driving axle. The engine, needless to say, would be motionless during this picturesque performance, and a more commonplace but more reliable one would have to assist her out of the station.

The object of this arrangement of uncoupled wheels was to produce the supposed free-running qualities of the single driver with the better adhesion of the coupled engine, but its principal results were exhibitions such as that just described. It was tried once more in England after Webb abandoned it, though with simple expansion, by Dugald Drummond on the South Western, in half-a-dozen 4–2, 2–0 engines built from 1897 on. The South Western and the Southern after it, incidentally, always described these engines officially as 4–2–2's. A number of Webb's variety was built for various foreign railways, from India to South America and the United States. Nobody was bitten twice, though the Oudh and Rohilkund Railway let itself in for a batch of ten.

After producing the John Hicks, Webb went over to coupled wheels and four-cylinder compounds, using the 4–4–0 type for passenger and the 0–8–0 and 4–6–0 types for goods traffic. The four-cylinder passenger engines were more reliable than the three-cylinder types, though sluggish and uneconomically complicated. George Whale, on succeeding Webb, scrapped all the three-cylinder passenger classes and rebuilt the goods and many of the four-cylinder. The first four-cylinder simple engines for regular main-line service in Britain were James Manson's No. 11, a Glasgow and South-Western 4–4–0 built in 1897, and Dugald Drummond's No. 720 for the London and South Western, the first of the 4–2, 2–0's previously mentioned. Both suffered from insufficient boiler power. The initial

On the "Cuckoo" line from Hailsham to Eridge, London, Brighton and South Coast Railway, about 1885. The engine is a late Jenny Lind type, built by J. C. Craven in 1862; the leading carriage is a Stroudley saloon with Cleminson radial trucks, built in 1881. There was no daytime headcode on the branch

L.S.W.R. engine was given a much larger boiler in 1905 and the G.S.W.R. engine was twice rebuilt, the last time with a very large boiler which made an excellent job of her.

The second important compounding system adopted in Victorian England was T. W. Worsdell's two-cylinder arrangement on the Great Eastern and North Eastern Railways, taken up by Malcolm on the Northern Counties. It was less eccentric than Webb's but did not last in England. Most successful was the Smith three-cylinder arrangement, in which the Webb sequence was reversed, a single inside high-pressure cylinder being used, with two outside low-pressure, and coupled wheels. In 1898 Wilson Worsdell on the North Eastern converted a two-cylinder compound 4–4–0 engine, No. 1619, to the Smith arrangement, in which form it worked quite successfully for very many years. During 1901–3, S. W. Johnson built five very fine Smith compound 4–4–0's, the first of the celebrated "Midland Compounds" already referred to, and the design was modified to its final form by R. M. Deeley in 1905. In the Smith and Smith-Deeley compounds, the engine could be worked as simple, semi-compound or full compound, simple expansion being employed on starting and semi-compound working, in which a limited amount of auxiliary high-pressure steam was admitted to the low-pressure steam chest, when the engine was heavily loaded or climbing. As mentioned in particular connection with the Midland Railway, the 4–4–0 three-cylinder compounds of that company had a very long and honourable career in express passenger service, and the L.M.S. added considerably to their numbers, years after their first appearance.

It is now necessary to turn back to consider the remarkable revival of express engines with single driving wheels during the 'eighties and 'nineties. Apart from some exceptional broad-gauge engines on the Great Western, the eight-wheel bogie single with inside cylinders made its first appearance with the two engines on the Great Northern Railway of Ireland, mentioned already, closely followed in 1886 by the solitary No. 123 on the Caledonian Railway. S. W. Johnson, who had introduced the standard-gauge inside-cylinder 4–4–0 bogie engine to England, after its previous appearance in Scotland, did the same for the inside-cylinder bogie single, putting the first into service on the Midland Railway in 1887. Unlike the Caledonian engine of the previous year, it had double frames and outside bearings, except for the leading bogie. Between 1887 and 1901, 95 Johnson singles, of several varieties, were built for the Midland Railway, with driving wheels ranging from 7 ft. 4 in. to 7 ft. 9½ in. The later examples were among the finest singles ever built. The design was copied on a more modest scale by James Holden on the Great Eastern.

Bogie singles with inside cylinders and frames were built by the North Eastern, Great Central and Great Northern Railways; in the last instance, H. A. Ivatt had produced an enlargement of Patrick Stirling's inside-cylinder 2–2–2's, adding a bogie. Dean on the Great Western Railway stuck to double frames, bogies also having outside frames and bearings. He had for some time remained wedded to the 2–2–2 type until, directly as a result of a derailment with the 2–2–2 engine *Wigmore Castle* in Box Tunnel, he began in 1894 the magnificent series of bogie singles always pre-eminently associated with his name.

During the 'nineties and early nineteen-hundreds, many of these "modern" singles did very excellent work on the various main lines, but theirs was a relatively brief, dragonfly existence in British express service. As a group, the Midland engines survived longest; the last to remain in service, however, was the ancient Caledonian No. 123, which after years of working the officers' saloon, returned to fast passenger traffic on the lightly loaded Perth and Dundee trains in 1930 and was withdrawn for preservation in 1935.

Easily the most widely used express engine during our period was the 4–4–0, usually with inside cylinders except in the case of compound engines and of those built by Adams on the London and South Western and Jones on the Highland. In his 1869 class on the North-Eastern, built in 1896, Wilson Worsdell used 7 ft. 7½ in. coupled wheels, but the usual diameter was around 6 ft. 6 in. for fast main-line work, increased to 7 ft.

on certain lines, and reduced to 6 ft. on mountainous railways such as the Highland.

It was on the Highland Railway that David Jones introduced the 4–6–0 type, long employed in America, to British railway practice. His big goods engine made its appearance in 1894, when it was the largest and most powerful locomotive in the country. It was a fall from the tender of one of these engines that incapacitated their designer when he was already working on a large passenger engine, designed on similar lines. As already recorded, it was left to his successor, Peter Drummond, to finish this with slight modifications, thus producing the celebrated Castle class of 1900. In the same year Wilson Worsdell on the North Eastern introduced the 4–6–0 express engine to England.

Of great antiquity was the 0–4–2 type. Two engineers revived it for main-line work in the late nineteenth century, Stroudley on the London, Brighton and South Coast with his 6 ft. 6 in. Richmond and Gladstone class express engines of 1878 and 1882 respectively, and Adams on the London and South Western with his Jubilee mixed traffics, having 6 ft. 1 in. coupled wheels. The only other 0–4–2 locomotives with such large coupled wheels were a class built by Kessler of Esslingen for the Galician Karl-Ludwigsbahn in the 'seventies, which, unlike the English engines, had outside cylinders and were decidedly nose-heavy. No such trouble assailed the Gladstones on the fastest Brighton trains.

Features of modern locomotive design which appeared during last century included the flat-top Belpaire firebox, brought to England from Belgium and incorporated in some engines built by Beyer, Peacock and Co. for the Malines–Terneuzen Railway in 1872, though it did not appear on the home railways until 1897, with Dean's Badmintons. Walschaert's valve gear, also Belgian, was experimentally employed by Robert Fairlie, who for years tried to popularize double-bogie locomotives, and appeared in a curious 0–4–4 tank engine built under his patents. This, probably the same as an engine shown at the Paris Exhibition of 1878, was rashly bought by the Swindon,

Marlborough and Andover Railway (later Midland and South Western Junction) in 1881. For years the engine—and the gear—were regarded as oddities not to be touched if anything else could be got to do the necessary work. In the end, Bowman Malcolm took up the gear on the Northern Counties and at long last it became a characteristic feature of modern British design. It was Malcolm, also, who first adopted the now universal Ross Pop safety valve, early in the present century.

Returning to our necessarily brief sketch of locomotive types, the Altantic, or 4–4–2 engine made its first British appearance under Ivatt on the Great Northern, with his "Klondykes" of 1898. The later, large-boilered Ivatt Atlantics, somewhat modified and fitted with superheaters, were destined to perform some of the finest work of their day; in the 1914–18 war they handled with ease and expedition immensely long trains, out of all proportion to their relatively low tractive effort. Aspinall on the Lancashire and Yorkshire adopted the 4–4–2 type a year after Ivatt, using inside cylinders, but the outside-cylinder variety was the one commonly used by other companies in emulation of the Great Northern, namely, the North Eastern (Wilson Worsdell, 1903), the Great Central (J. G. Robinson, 1903), the Great Western (G. J. Churchward, 1905), the North British (W. P. Reid, 1906), and the London, Brighton and South Coast (D. E. Marsh, 1907). A number of De Glehn four-cylinder compound Atlantics was built experimentally, of which the best known were three on the Great Western. These, built at Belfort, were originally entirely French in design apart from their standard Great Western tenders. The home-produced Great Western Atlantics had a short career as such, and were converted to the 4–6–0 type.

One of the very important innovations in locomotive design made during the first decade of this century was the introduction of the smoke-tube superheater. Many designs were brought out based on the original work of Schmidt in Germany. The Schmidt superheater made its British debut on two goods engines of the Lancashire and Yorkshire Railway, so equipped by George Hughes in 1906. Two years later D. E. Marsh on the Brighton fitted it to his new 4–4–2 express tank engines. Two of these, Nos. 21 and 26, worked unofficial trials turn and turnabout with Whale's Precursor class 4–4–0 *Titan* of the London and North Western, on the Sunny South Special between Brighton and Rugby. So striking were the results shown by the Brighton engines that Crewe was obliged to take notice. The immediate outcome was the George the Fifth class on the L.N.W.R., and a general adoption of superheating by the British main-line railways. Excellent variations of this period, on Schmidt's original theme, were Robinson's superheater on the Great Central and Churchward's Swindon superheater on the Great Western.

The considerable success of various relatively small 4–4–0 and 0–6–0 passenger and goods engines during the early years of the present century, compared with very similar engines built during the 'eighties and early 'nineties, was due to something which happened on the Caledonian Railway in 1896. J. F. McIntosh was the C.R. locomotive superintendent at that time. He was a character with a pawky wit, piercing eyes and only one hand, together with the more important capacity for using other people's brains. For the Caledonian, he built characteristic Drummond-type locomotives, with a memorable difference. His works manager, Robert Urie, is said to have suggested: "Why not build the same engine with a much bigger boiler?" The result of whatever really happened was the celebrated Dunalastair class of 1896. These were essentially the same as Drummond's and Lambie's 4–4–0 locomotives that had gone before, but with 4 ft. 8 in. diameter boilers. The first Dunalastair series had 1,402·3 sq. ft. of heating surface and the second Dunalastairs of 1897, 1,500 sq. ft. compared with 1,208·6 sq. ft. on Drummond's Carbrook class. So successful were the results of McIntosh's work that during the nineteen-hundreds the capacity of locomotives to generate steam steadily increased instead of remaining static or, as in the case of Stirling's engines on the Great Northern, growing "little by little and beautifully less."*

* Acknowledgement to the late E. L. Ahrons.

The most famous engines of McIntosh's design, that magnificent *Cardean*, already mentioned, and her sisters, were simply enlarged, elongated, six-coupled Dunalastairs. During the first decade of this century, several very large locomotives made their appearance on both English and Scottish railways. Dugald Drummond's 330 class four-cylinder 4–6–0's on the London and South-Western were, at the time of their appearance in 1905, the largest express engines in the country. To this, a qualification should be added. They were by no means successful engines and did little passenger work on the Salisbury–Exeter line for which they had been designed. Of far greater importance was the work of G. J. Churchward of the Great Western, whose Star class four-cylinder 4–6–0's were in their day second to none in Britain. Churchward used for the Stars what was then the very high working pressure of 225 lb. per sq. in., with long laps and long valve travel; these features, combined by R. E. L. Maunsell with a high degree of superheat, after the close of our period, on the South Eastern and Chatham Railway, produced the modern main-line locomotive of our own time.

In 1908, Churchward went a step further, by producing the first British 4–6–2 express engine, G.W.R. No. 111, *The Great Bear*. She was, it might be said, a "Super Star," or, if her name be a guide, and forgetting some aeroplanes recently much discussed, a Constellation. The Stars, however, were the really successful engines; *The Great Bear*, owing to serious restrictions in running, was confined to the Paddington-Bristol line, and remained an isolated engine. In 1924, C. B. Collett scrapped her, the number and, presumably, the goodwill of the engine passing to a new Castle class 4–6–0, the logical development of the Stars. Her big watercart bogie tender was used for some time with one of Churchward's County class 4–4–0's and ended its days during the late war as a static water tank in front of Swindon Works.

During this period, a number of locomotive exchanges took place between the various main-line railways, with a view to comparing locomotive results. The comparative running of the North Western *Titan* and the London, Brighton and South

Coast 4–4–2 tanks has already been mentioned. A startling feature of this was that, while *Titan* had to make a water-stop at Willesden, the Brighton engines, in spite of their limited tank capacity, ran easily from Rugby to East Croydon without watering. Moreover, unlike the North Western engine, they were not fitted with scoops and therefore could not supplement their ration on watertroughs.

When a Great Western Star was exchanged with a North Western Precursor, the latter provided no comparison at all with the Great Western engine. The remarkable work of the latter induced C. J. Bowen Cooke of the North Western to design his four-cylinder 4–6–0 express engines of the Sir Gilbert Claughton class in 1913. Though built under Great Western influence, the Claughtons exemplified Crewe practice as much as all their predecessors. Just as, in appearance, a North-Western Prince might be described as a much-enlarged, superheated Ramsbottom engine, so was the Claughton easily and quite reasonably to be likened to a giant simple-expansion six-coupled version of Webb's Alfred the Great class four-cylinder compound 4–4–0's. They were unfortunately disappointing engines, with insufficient boiler power. A few were given larger boilers by the L.M.S., but most were ruthlessly scrapped and replaced under that company by the excellent Patriot or "Baby Scot" class three-cylinder 4–6–0 design.

For the most part, during the nineteen hundreds, many suburban services in the London area and elsewhere were being handled by small 2–4–2 or 0–4–4 tank engines, and these, indeed, were retained in general service until the slow advance of electrification superseded them. An interesting experiment was, however, carried out on the Great Eastern Railway in 1902. The company was being threatened with competition by a rival scheme for an electric railway to the north-eastern suburbs, which promised a much more expeditious service. James Holden, the Great Eastern locomotive superintendent, who deputed much of his work, accordingly required the late Fred V. Russell to prepare a suburban tank engine capable of accelerating a standard Great Eastern suburban train to the legended figure of "30 m.p.h. in 30 seconds." The result was the three-cylinder Decapod No. 20, throughout our period the only ten-coupled engine to run on a British railway.

This Decapod, with the unprecedented total heating surface of 3,010 sq. ft. and 200 lb. pressure, did all that was required of her in the way of demonstration, and the proposed electric railway came to nothing. But, having exhibited her powers, Decapod came to nothing also. The Great Eastern, unwilling to rebuild dozens of structures to take such heavy engines on its suburban lines, went on as before, and the big engine was scrapped after a short life converted into an 0–8–0 goods with a much smaller boiler.

This was the first modern three-cylinder simple locomotive in Great Britain. The arrangement was later extensively taken up for main-line service. On the Great Central in 1909, J. G. Robinson rebuilt one of his Atlantics as a three-cylinder simple, but the most successful early application of this type was by Vincent Raven on the North Eastern Railway from 1911 onwards. Previously, in 1907, Robinson had used three simple-expansion cylinders for his heavy 0–8–4 tanks used for humping in Wath yards, and before Raven produced his three-cylinder express engine he also had applied the arrangement to heavy goods and shunting tanks.

The eight-coupled goods locomotive, as remarked in a previous chapter, made its first appearance in Britain with the Swedish and Norwegian engines acquired by the Barry Railway. For tank locomotives the type, though rare in the old days, was of decided antiquity. The Avonside Engine Company had built it for the Vale of Neath and the Great Northern Railways in 1864 and 1866. But the 0–8–0 tender engine made its debut on the Barry as late as 1889. In 1892, the inside-cylinder 0–8–0 goods made its initial appearance on the London and North Western Railway, to be taken up later by the Caledonian, the Hull and Barnsley, the Lancashire and Yorkshire, and the Great Northern ("Long Toms"). The outside-cylinder type was adopted by the Great Central ("Pompoms") and North

Eastern Railways. In 1901 Webb on the North-Western produced four-cylinder compound 0–8–0 coal engines, but his inside-cylinder type, subject to enlargement, remained the standard North Western heavy goods for the rest of the company's separate existence.

The outside-cylinder 2–8–0 goods, long used in America, made its British entry under Churchward of the Great Western in 1903. The most widely-known variety was that of Robinson, first built for the Great Central in 1911, which was adopted as the standard military engine for British Army use in the 1914–18 war. Since then, in war and peace, these Great Central type engines have found their way far across the world; some of the war veterans eventually turned up in China, while others served again in the war just past, notably in the Middle East. The last classes of this type to come within our period were Gresley's on the Great Northern, brought out in 1913, and a series built at Derby for the Somerset and Dorset Joint Railway in the following year.

Eight-coupled locomotives were rare in the South of England, except on the Great Western, for there were none of the heavy mineral hauls such as demanded their services in the North and from South Wales. There were the Somerset and Dorset engines mentioned above, and *Hecate*, a solitary 0–8–0 tank on the Kent and East Sussex Railway. The South Eastern and the Brighton relied on the 0–6–0, and the South-Western used 4–6–0's for its heavy night goods trains, a practice largely maintained to this day by the Southern Railway.

Two remarkable tank locomotive classes should be mentioned, both built by Beyer, Peacock and Company for the steeply graded underground line of the Mersey Railway between Liverpool and Birkenhead. The older, 0–6–4 side-tanks with double frames and outside cranks, were among the most powerful locomotives in Great Britain when they appeared in 1885. Two years later came a 2–6–2 tank design, based on Beyer Peacock's standard 2–6–0 tender engine for colonial and South American service, with outside cylinders. On the electrification of the Mersey Railway in 1902, some of these heavy and powerful tank engines found their way far afield, even to industrial service in Australia.

All through railway history, engineers have endeavoured at intervals to provide something in the nature of a self-propelled railcar for passenger service on lightly laid branches having limited traffic. Bridges Adams made some remarkable attempts right back in the 'forties, and in 1869 George England built, at Hatcham Ironworks, Old Kent Road, the first British example of the double-bogie steam rail motor. Nothing more of the kind happened for over 30 years thereafter, then, in 1903, Dugald Drummond placed two in service on the L.S.W. and L.B.S.C. joint line between Fratton and East Southsea. They consisted of very small 0–2–2 locomotives with (originally) vertical boilers, to which were articulated long saloon coach bodies, four-wheel bogies supporting the outer ends. Many varieties were built by the British railway companies during the nineteen-hundreds, some with vertical boilers, notably on the Great Western, others of more orthodox railway type; some had single driving wheels, most were four-coupled, and one, on the Port Talbot, six-coupled.

The disadvantage of these, of their ancient predecessors, and of their much more modern successors like the Sentinel and Clayton geared steam railcars built for the L.M.S. and L.N.E.R. in the nineteen-twenties, was always the same; the unit was not sufficiently versatile. Engine and car were affected by one another's ailments. With extra traffic, the machine must have a trailer, cramping its rather inadequate style, or else be laid off in favour of an ordinary train, an uneconomic proceeding. The push-and-pull unit, using a small tank engine with reasonable reserve power, was found to possess most of its advantages without the drawbacks, indeed, the pioneer Drummond came to this conclusion in 1906, though he spoilt its effect by building very small locomotives with scarcely more power reserve than the motor engines themselves.

A few concluding notes on features of locomotive design: Throughout our period, designers were sharply divided as to whether boilers should supply steam from a dome, or whether this mounting was of negligible value. The Stirlings, Hugh Smellie, and G. J. Churchward had little use for the dome. Churchward favoured the Belpaire firebox, serving the same purpose with its wide, square steam-space above, and all used a perforated pipe for steam collection. Churchward's predecessor on the Great Western, William Dean, built some engines domeless and others, as if to make up for it, with very large domes. Stroudley began his Brighton career with domeless engines, but abandoned them almost at once.

Top feed, in which feedwater entering the boiler was partly purified by being injected at the top and falling down into the boiler through a series of removable trays, first applied on the Bergisch-Märkische Railway in Germany during the 'sixties, was introduced to England by Churchward on the Great Western, and later spread to many other lines.

The common British tender was six-wheeled, with outside frames and bearings, and the springs easily accessible outside the frames above the axleboxes. It owed its application on a large scale to Joseph Beattie of the London and South Western during the 'fifties, and is now one of the most old-fashioned features of ordinary British locomotives, though its qualities are undoubted. James Stirling on the South Eastern for long continued to use an older form of six-wheel tender, narrow in the body, with the springs above the platforms on each side. Likewise Webb on the North Western always used a very antiquated type of tender with wooden frames, at least partly on the grounds that in collision the timber broke up easily and formed a shock absorber between engine and train.

For many of his Brighton engines, Stroudley placed the tender springs and bearings inside, a pretty arrangement, which, however, made them very inaccessible for examination or repair. On certain lines where water-troughs were few or non-existent (they were invented by Ramsbottom of the North-Western and first laid down as far back as 1860) bogie tenders were used, as on most foreign railways. Dugald and Peter Drummond, on the L.S.W. and the Highland Railways, used inside-framed bogies, having the same disadvantage as

Stroudley's arrangement on the Brighton. McIntosh on the Caledonian and Manson on the Glasgow and South Western had the tender bogie frames outside in their large express engines.

On the London, Brighton and South Coast Railway, there was latterly an increasing tendency to discard tenders altogether, owing to the short, fast hauls which were a feature of that railway. We have already seen how Marsh's 4-4-2 tanks consumed far less water between Croydon and Rugby than Whale's Precursor class engine, which had to make an extra water-stop. Marsh's two 4-6-2 express tank engines of 1912, and Lawson Billinton's 4-6-4 tank design of 1914, were magnificent engines in their day. Even at the time of writing, Marsh's beautiful *Bessborough*, as Southern Railway No. 2326, takes me daily to my place of business, reprieved from the scrap siding where she spent a year or so, and superbly re-adorned in glittering bright green paint.

That must be our survey of British locomotives between 1874 and 1914, an abridgement of an abridgement. For a fuller picture, readers are recommended to consult the various specialized histories and the late E. L. Ahron's monumental work.* As a complement to the present chapter, some leading dimensions of characteristic engines built during the 40 years covered will be found in Appendix A at the end.

* *The British Steam Railway Locomotive*, 1825-1925 by the late E. L. Ahrons, M.I.Mech.E., M.I.Loco.E. (Locomotive Publishing Co., Limited, 1927).

# CHAPTER SEVEN

# CARRIAGES, GOOD AND BAD

"WHY on earth," said my colleague who had graduated in the steps of Stroudley, "are you making all this fuss about the old Brighton Pullmans? What's a coach, anyway? It's only a box on wheels!"

That, I retorted, was evidently a very common point of view on the London, Brighton and South Coast, judging by what one often had to ride in. Still, Stroudley could and did build a few very good vehicles, apart from the superb Pullman cars, which were imported from America. Now, no apology is made, and sympathetic attention is claimed, for a very pet subject of the present author is the railway carriage.

Its lineage is ancient. The characteristic British arrangement of side doors with droplights and quarter lights on each side, goes back to the seventeenth century, to a time when Sir Isaac Newton's rather premature plan for a jet-propelled kettle on wheels was the nearest approach yet to a locomotive. Among its ancestors the British railway carriage numbers the stage coach, the family carriage and the sedan chair. The saloon carriage of Victorian days was of more original conception, but it numbered the horse wagonette among its forbears; likewise the American type of coach, whence was derived the Pullman car, owed something to the omnibus and the old Yankee canal boat.

In our opening chapter we have seen what the very best type of English express train was like in the middle of the 'seventies, with Clayton's bogie carriages and American Pullman sleeping cars. In 1874 the Midland had indeed attempted to introduce the American style of car for all classes, with centre-gangway day coaches for third class and for the moribund second, and parlour and sleeping cars for the first. But the general public would not be directed, and only the luxurious varieties were retained. The Midland train of 1876, which we encountered in Chapter One, would look antiquated to-day, yet somehow familiar in its leading features. The worst type of train from the same decade would look, thank heavens, most unfamiliar. In 1876, alone in Europe, the Midland Railway carried all its third-class passengers in decent, civilized, upholstered carriages. True, the Great Western had ordinary carriages as good as those of the Midland, and very similar in appearance, but second class was its nearest approach to affording comfortable travel to those of moderate means; some of the Great Western thirds, then and for many years after, compared nicely with the most picturesquely disgraceful antiques mustered by the South Eastern.

Back in 1874, the ordinary British railway carriage was four- or six-wheeled. The Metropolitan Railway used non-bogie eight-wheelers, a type built experimentally by the Great Western as far back as 1852 (the "Long Charleys"); the latter company had a solitary bogie first class running on the Paddington–Birkenhead line; the Great Northern had a design for a bogie composite, but did not carry it any further. There were, except on the exclusive Pullman cars, no corridors, lavatories, radiator heating, or any artificial light save that of the primeval oil-pot in the roof on ordinary main-line carriages. The District, Metropolitan, North London, and Lancashire and Yorkshire, however, used coal gas in collapsible holders, carried in oblong roof boxes of clerestory shape on the London underground lines, and in the guards' vans on the others. Two gas-jet globes was the allowance in a Metropolitan or District first class, and a gushing contemporary account described the result as so brilliant as to destroy all suggestion of travelling underground.

The roofs were of plain camber shape, nearly flat and equipped with luggage rails in the oldest carriages. The curved, three-cornered window, another relic of ancient road practice, was still to be seen, but had become unfashionable in the 'sixties. First class was of the ordinary type with three well-cushioned seats each side, divided by headrests and elbows. The latter were usually fixed, so it was not possible to fold them up and stretch out when the train was lightly loaded at night; otherwise, first-class travel was by no means bad. Second-class compartments had the seats thinly padded and covered with corded velveteen or American cloth, and often two compartments had to share one oil-pot lamp, occupying a half-moon hole cut in the top of the intervening partition. The third-class compartments were generally mean, wooden, and with partitions carried barely to shoulder height. This assisted general sociability, and also favoured the wandering minstrel on an excursion train or the travelling evangelist trying to save souls by the way.

Brakes were often hand-operated, and dependent on vans marshalled at strategic intervals along the train. Certain lines used early types of continuous brakes, chiefly mechanical in principle, such as Clarke's and Clarke and Webb's chain brakes on the North London and the London and North Western Railways, applied by rotation of the axles on engagement of a clutch. The Lancashire and Yorkshire used Fay's brake and the Highland employed Newall's, on their steeply graded lines, both arrangements operated by hand wheels through longitudinal rotating shafts under the carriages, with jointed couplings between each vehicle. Of power brakes—pneumatic, vacuum and hydraulic—the Westinghouse air system was most promising, and gave a very good showing on a Midland train at the famous Newark brake trials during June 1875. It was automatic in action and brought a train weighing 203.2 tons with engine, from 52 m.p.h. to a stand in 19 seconds and 913 ft. from time and point of application. None of the mechanical brakes was automatic. They were useless for arresting vehicles which broke away from their controlling van.

In the early 'seventies, extra travelling comfort could be had at a price. For wealthy invalids, the South Eastern Railway had built, as far back as 1860, a carriage with a movable bed and a fully equipped lavatory, and during the middle 'sixties, various companies began to provide family carriages, available on payment of a certain number of first- or first and second-class fares. Usually there would be comfortable armchair- or cross-seats for the Governor and Mamma, and less easy ones along the sides for their brood and for poor Miss Jones. Adjacently there would be a lavatory, complicated in equipment and floral in decoration, and beyond that a very small second class where John and Mary Anne sat in readiness to assist Master and Madame on the journey or at its end.

The very first British sleeping carriage, apart from invalid coaches and such makeshifts as twin sticks and a cushion placed between the seats, was a six-wheeler built by the North British Railway in 1873, for the East Coast night expresses. It was designed very much on family saloon lines, for it was considered that such intimate things as sleepers would be chiefly in demand by large family parties travelling together. There were two compartments, each with three high-back bed-chairs of a type previously introduced in France for the *lits-salon* and *coupé-lits* types. The beds were formed by pulling the high seatbacks forward and downwards. Seats and armrests folded up underneath and the user lay down on the reverse side of the back. The whole contraption was trimmed in crimson velvet, and passengers brought their own bedding if they wanted it. A short central corridor connected the two compartments, with a lavatory on one side and a separate W.C. on the other. At one end was a luggage compartment with double doors and at the other the inevitable servants' second class.

This *lits-salon* type of sleeping berth persisted on certain British railways into the 'eighties, side-by-side with the American Pullman type previously described, in which bedclothes were provided from the beginning. Pullman parlour cars appeared on the Midland Railway in 1874 along with the sleepers. They, likewise, were completely American except in their reduced dimensions, with a long general saloon furnished with pivoted easy chairs, one or two private compartments similarly equipped, lavatories and Baker hot-water heaters. Entrance to the Pullman cars was by open platforms at the ends, except on two special short-bodied centre-vestibule sleeping cars called *Balmoral* and *Dunrobin*, used on the Highland Railway from 1885 to 1907.

From the beginning, it had been possible to serve meals in

Midsummer Eve: The 2.0 p.m. Scotch express climbing from Beattock to the summit; Caledonian 4–6–0 locomotive No. 903, *Cardean*, with banking engine in the rear

the Pullman cars to passengers who ordered them in advance. The food usually arrived in baskets, but there were facilities for serving hot meals previously cooked and kept warm. In 1879, however, a Pullman car called *Prince of Wales* was placed in service on the Leeds expresses of the Great Northern Railway, and this contained a fully equipped kitchen, being thus the first real dining car in Great Britain. Passengers rode in it all the way, and paid a half-crown Pullman supplement for so doing, in addition to the price of meals.

Apart from the Pullman cars, there appeared in 1878 and 1881 respectively, two types of bogie sleeping car with the berths in compartments having lavatory access through side corridors. The earlier design, about which, unfortunately, little information has survived, was by David Jones for the Highland Railway, before the advent of the two Pullmans just referred to. There were three cars, apparently following a plan introduced to Continental Europe by W. D. Mann in 1871. The second design was carried out on the Great Western under William Dean, probably by James Holden, for the West of England night expresses, and formed in many important particulars the prototype of the modern British sleeping car. There was a side corridor throughout, in this example crossing over in the middle through a steward's pantry. All the berths were arranged in compartments, longitudinally at the ends but otherwise across the car, and there were no upper berths. The crossover corridor was supposed to secure a good balance. Ventilation was by ordinary droplights and by the deep, boxlike clerestory which was for so many years characteristic of the Great Western. This very fine sleeping carriage held twelve first-class passengers; the body, approximately 46½ ft. long by 9 ft. wide, was temporarily mounted on a broad-gauge frame and bogies. This was indeed the first narrow-body convertible broad-gauge carriage. Like ordinary Great Western first-class coaches of the period, it was handsomely furnished in morocco leather, heavily embossed lincrusta and gilt mouldings. Though pompous, the style was very superior to the florid glitter of contemporary Pullman cars; moreover, while on the Great Western, sleeping-car passengers had to provide their own bedding, at that time they paid no supplement for use of the berths.

Following this corridor sleeper on the Great Western, in 1882 the Great Northern Railway designed the first British side-corridor ordinary coach, a six-wheel first class for the East Coast Joint Stock. It had four compartments, each containing four seats. One was for ladies only, and had its own lavatory adjoining; there was a "gents" at the other end. There were as yet no gangway connection between carriages; as remarked, the first diner passengers travelled all the way in the same car. In 1888, a very similar Great Northern corridor coach design was brought out for third-class passengers, having five compartments. These two classes remained the standard for the East Coast Scotch expresses until the end of the century, with a few important exceptions.

Great improvements had been made in the dimensions of passenger compartments. In 1875, the Midland had fixed on 6 ft. as the minimum distance between partitions of a third-class compartment, and had discarded the very objectionable low partitions at the same time as upholstering the seats. First-class compartments varied from about 7 ft. to 7 ft. 6 in. between partitions.

During the 'eighties, bogie coaches appeared in increasing numbers on the best express trains of various railways in addition to the Great Western and the Midland, notably on the London and South Western, Manchester, Sheffield and Lincolnshire, North Eastern, and even on the despised and lampooned South Eastern, whereon the veteran Richard Mansell built them for the Dover Continental expresses. The Great Northern and the London and North Western were much more suspicious of the bogie coach. The former remained enamoured of its standard six-wheelers, while building a few eight-wheel non-bogie carriages. The North Western for long had its style cramped by an old short traverser at Euston. From the middle 'eighties onwards it built many eight-wheel carriages with the outer axles mounted on Webb's radial trucks. Webb claimed that these ran more smoothly and more steadily than bogie carriages, but his celebrated radials were prone to treat their passengers to sudden lurches at disconcerting moments. What was wanted at that time was a combination of Clayton's beautiful twelve-wheel Midland coaches and the North Western's magnificent permanent way.

One other form of flexible wheelbase deserves passing notice, the radial truck arrangement of James Cleminson. In this, used for six-wheel carriages, the middle axle was on a laterally sliding frame, connected by radial rods to a pair of pivoted trucks carrying the outer axles. It enjoyed little application except on several narrow-gauge railways. On the main lines, Jones of the Highland and Stroudley of the Brighton gave it a trial, but did not adopt it generally. It was used to some extent abroad.

So far, the bogie most in use on carriages had been the American type, built up of wood strengthened by flitchplates, with spiral springs bearing on a long outside compensating beam connecting the two axleboxes on each side, and with double laminated bolster springs. From the late 'eighties onwards, however, pressed steel bogie frames with ouside laminated springs over the axleboxes enjoyed a considerable vogue. A Midland twelve-wheel lavatory carriage by Clayton, mounted on this type of bogie, excited great admiration at the Paris Exhibition of 1889, and was awarded the *Grand Prix*. Certainly, no such superlatively good third-class accommodation had ever before been seen or even thought of in France, or, for that matter, anywhere else in Europe.

Provision of lavatories, with or without corridor access, now began to be more common on British express trains, though many lines continued to confine it to the first class. Some companies, notably the Cambrian, Caledonian and North British, were much concerned to ensure that the new lavatory carriages seated the same number of passengers per compartment as their predecessors. So the lavatory doors were padded, and hinged seats were placed in front of them. For sensitive people, especially ladies, it was a horrifying arrangement.

The 'eighties also saw gradual adoption on certain lines of

oil gas for lighting, the illuminant being carried in cylinders under the frames and used in fish-tail or, in the very best stock, in Argand annular burners. Stroudley on the Brighton from 1881 onwards, and Clayton on the Midland, made considerable use for some time of electric light, with storage cells charged, like the gas cylinders, at suitable times and places. The light, however, was little brighter than gas and much less steady; the old carbon-filament lamps were fragile and unreliable, and the batteries uneconomically heavy.

While dining service was at first provided exclusively by the Pullman cars, from the late 'eighties onwards several railway companies began to provide their own dining cars, notably the London and North Western, which never used Pullmans. Some very handsome twelve-wheel diners, for first-class only, were built by the Manchester, Sheffield and Lincolnshire Railway in 1888 (this company had built twelve-wheel ordinary coaches since 1885) and were operated by it jointly with the Great Northern Railway between Manchester and King's Cross via Retford.

But the most important contribution to dining-car services, after the original Pullman service on the Great Northern, was that of James Holden on the Great Eastern Railway in 1891. For its Harwich Continental service, this company put on a first and third-class dining-car train, which was also notable in that it was one of the first two sets of coaches in the country, apart from Pullmans, to be interconnected by covered gangways. There was a four-compartment first-class side-corridor coach, then a dining-saloon to seat eighteen, with a kitchen at one end, and to complete the set, a third-class side-corridor coach with five compartments, one of which had a table and tip-up seats. All were six-wheelers; the middle vehicle had the sides bulged out to give greater elbow room to the hungry diners who had survived the crossing from Holland without permanent prostration, and a clerestory roof. Cooking and lighting were by oil gas. If not an immensely imposing sort of train, it was nevertheless a very noteworthy one and provides a landmark in the history of passenger amenities. The short-bodied dining saloons were later greatly enlarged and mounted on six-wheel bogies, in which form they gave useful service for many years. A curiosity about the third class was that its "ladies only" compartment had lavatory access only, and was cut off from the main corridor.

In the same year of 1891, the Great Western built what is generally regarded as the prototype of the modern British corridor train. It consisted of five vehicles, all mounted on Dean's four-wheel bogies, which had four-point suspension by pendulum links with the central pin acting as a guide only. There was a guard's brake and luggage van, a third class, a first, a second and a brake third. All the four passenger-carrying vehicles had oil-gas lighting, clerestory roofs and the sides bulged out between the flat doors in a style known on the Great Western as the "bay window" type. Men's and women's lavatories were separate, at opposite ends of the carriages. Side corridors were used except for the smoking compartments, which had open passageways with cross seats on each side, as in a diner.

The flexible bellows connections between carriages were at one side instead of centrally-placed, which meant that the train had to remain permanently marshalled as a block set. This gangway arrangement persisted for several years on Great Western corridor stock, and is retained to this day for Travelling Post Office carriages, which ply on regular and invariable routes. For passenger stock, of course, it had awkward results when a vehicle was turned on a triangular junction in the normal course of operations.

The Great Western corridor train, after some experimental runs, went into regular service between Paddington and Birkenhead in 1892 and was an immediate success. It did not include a dining car; the corridors were intended simply to give complete lavatory access and to enable the guard to patrol the whole train while running. He held the key to the gangway connections which he kept locked to prevent third-class passengers from moving into superior quarters on the quiet. The credit for having produced the typical British express train of later years may therefore be shared jointly by the old Great Eastern, with its

York Continental, and the Great Western with its Birkenhead Corridor, both built in the same year.

A most interesting feature of the Great Western train was its system of passengers' communication. On most British railways at that time, this was a very weak point, in spite of the periodic incidence of criminal attacks and assaults in isolated compartments. The commonest arrangement was the rigging of a cord through eyelets outside the carriage, on the gutter rail. This communication cord was coupled between the carriages, with a good deal of slack, and operated a gong or a whistle on the locomotive. In the van, the other end of the cord was wound on a sort of winch with a large wheel rather like a ship's. It had been devised on the North Eastern Railway and generally applied on railways north of the Thames from 1869 onwards. This served its purpose after a fashion, but using it in sudden emergency was an awkward business. The passenger faced with abrupt murderous attack, or a girl at the mercy of a ruffian, had to remember quickly which was the right side of the rapidly moving train, open the window, grope upwards for the elusive cord and pull in several feet of slack before anything happened. Sometimes the cord stuck or broke, and nothing happened at all. In a bad smash on the Great Western (Shipton, on Christmas Eve of 1874), a passenger, previously becoming alarmed at the violent motion of his carriage, leant out of the window to get at the cord and was thrown through it on to the grass by a violent lurch. He was unhurt, saved by the accident of an accident, for the train turned over immediately after, with heavy loss of life.

On the Great Western corridor train just described, electric bells were provided in all compartments, by which the guard could be summoned from his van. Outside the carriages, in the same place as the usual cord, there was a wire, which on being pulled, made a partial application of the automatic vacuum brake. This, of course, is the principle of the present arrangement, with a tight chain inside the carriages and an external disc or semaphore indicator at the end. It was officially approved and generally adopted on all main-line British and Irish railways from 1899 onwards, being applicable to either the Westinghouse or the vacuum automatic brake. On open electric stock, a turncock in the air-pipe serves the same function.

Long before this, the much maligned southern lines had done far more enterprising things than the northern companies in the cause of emergency communication, using various electrical systems. The best was Stroudley and Rusbridge's patent electric arrangement on the London, Brighton and South Coast, operated by a pull-out knob in a conspicuous position on the compartment partition. It survived on the older Brighton carriages right into the nineteen-twenties.

From the early 'nineties onwards, corridor coaches were employed to an increasing extent on the best expresses. On the West Highland trains of the North British, and on the American boat expresses of the London and South Western, central corridors were employed, without end gangways. The South Eastern Railway, in 1892, had a train of first-class drawing-room cars built in America by the Gilbert Car Manufacturing Company of Troy. They were of Pullman type, with open platforms at the ends, but previously, on the London, Brighton and South Coast in 1889, Pullman cars with closed vestibules had made their appearance on the Brighton Limited trains. In 1897, the South Eastern Railway had built in England a really magnificent eight-car centre-corridor train, very much on American lines, with closed vestibules and flexible connections throughout. There was a first-class drawing-room with a first-class pantry car, a second class and five third class including the brake thirds at the ends. The underframes were composite, with the solebars of steel, there were Gould automatic centre-couplers between the coaches, electric lighting with dynamos and closed-circuit hot-water heating with a stove to each vehicle. There were clerestories over all the passenger sections, but on the brake thirds the luggage compartments had plain roofs, with raised lookouts for the guard, giving an up and down effect and spoiling the appearance of what was otherwise the finest complete train in the country. This American Car Train, as it was called, was placed in service on the Charing Cross–Hastings service, but the incalculable British public did not take to it.

The train suffered the same luke-warm reception as had the Midland American trains of the 'seventies. It was complained that the carriages were too warm, or too draughty, or that they afforded no privacy. These objections came rather oddly from a public which, on the South Eastern, had been using some of the poorest third-class stock in the country. Nevertheless, the cars were dispersed and taken over by the Pullman company, which used them singly on various trains.

Dining-car trains for all classes of passenger, initiated as we have seen by the Great Eastern Railway, made their appearance on the Anglo-Scottish expresses of the Midland, East Coast and West Coast companies in 1893, though at first only the West Coast Joint Stock provided complete corridor trains. An excellent feature of the East Coast expresses, which were of Great Northern design, was the provision of a separate kitchen car, six-wheeled in this case, marshalled between the first- and the third-class diners, thus providing centralized cooking and, in the passenger quarters, relative freedom from the greasy nidor of different viands being prepared together in a confined space. The Midland and West Coast companies used twelve-wheel dining cars with kitchens included.

In that same year of 1893, the Chicago World Fair was in full blast, and to it the London and North Western sent the Webb three-cylinder compound 2–2, 2–2 engine *Queen Empress*, together with a standard sleeping car and a lavatory-composite coach, both bogie eight-wheelers. The sleeper had the berths arranged longitudinally in cabins, on a plan which enjoyed some popularity in the 'nineties. Common American opinions were, on the whole, distinguished by critical amusement; it was impossible to take seriously main-line stock which had no through passageway of any kind. The carriages were decorated with, among other abominations, pokerwork panels representing Truth and Justice. Decorative taste as exemplified in the Pullman and Wagner "palace cars" on contemporary American railways was, if anything, worse. But it was much richer and more costly, so Truth and Justice somehow failed to impress even the Philistine.

After exhibition, the "English Train" ran from Chicago to New York under its own steam, with some Wagner sleeping cars in rear of the two London and North Western vehicles. For this journey, to conform with Federal law, the engine had an American locomotive bell mounted on the tender and a powerful headlamp lashed somewhat lopsidedly to her buffer-beam. An illustration of this North Western train, standing in Grand Central Station, New York, was published in *Locomotive Engineering* (New York) for February, 1894.

During the 'nineties, in spite of the example of the Great Western Railway, odd and various designs of sleeping car still served the three main lines between England and Scotland, indeed, the Midland Railway, though it had by then bought all the old Pullman cars into its own stock, continued building that type of vehicle right up to 1900. The East Coast companies, and then the West Coast, took up the side-corridor sleeper with lower berths only, the East Coast building exclusively single-berth compartment cars, each with one or two double-berth compartments. Great Northern external conventions were followed, though David Bain, then on the North-Eastern and later of the Midland, was largely responsible for the best East Coast Joint carriages at this time. With end doors, Pullman vestibules and Gould couplers, and clerestory roofs, the cars had a certain American flavour about their external appearance. C. A. Park of the London and North Western built similar vehicles for the West Coast, though he never adopted the automatic coupler and Pullman vestibule.

Passing reference has already been made to periodic progress in the heating and lighting of carriages. As far back as 1843, hot-water heating, or rather the admission of air-preheated by a closed circuit hot-water coil with a small boiler under the vehicle, had been devised by Perkins (of steam gun notoriety) and installed in the London and Birmingham Railway's royal saloon, but at the beginning of our period and for many years after, the flat hot-water tin on the floor was the only apparatus available to prevent ordinary passengers freezing on winter journeys. The tins left much to be desired; when freshly installed they induced heat-ache in the feet, when they cooled they became a useless clutter on the floor. At one stage in the history of British fashion, boots with gutta-percha soles came into favour. These stuck to the carriage footwarmers, and left their wearers effectively birdlimed. In 1880, on the London and North Western, F. W. Webb introduced tins containing sodium acetate. Heated in a boiling vat on the platform, this liquified, and on solidifying again it gave out the heat it had previously absorbed, continuing to do so for as long as any of the salts remained uncrystalized. One could give new life to the expiring footwarmer by giving it a violent shaking, and even on a long night journey it was good for several hours.

On the old Pullman cars, as already recorded, the American Baker heater was in use, somewhat resembling the ordinary greenhouse apparatus, with a small oil-fired boiler and hot-water pipes making a circuit of the car. The West Lancashire, as already remarked, used steam heat with a boiler in the van from 1879 on. Another glimmer of things to come was seen in the late 'eighties, when the Caledonian Railway diverted the exhaust steam from the locomotive's Westinghouse brake pump to heat radiators in the carriages. It was a makeshift; the flexible connections between the carriages were made out of hosepipe which had become too worn to serve more serious purposes. In it, however, was the main principal of modern heating by low-pressure steam.

On the Glasgow and South Western Railway at the same time, there was a very clever heating system operated on the something-for-nothing principle. Above the flame of the carriage lamp there was a small wrought-iron boiler, serving a closed pipe circuit incorporating a sort of heat reservoir under one of the seats. If the lamps were unlit, the passengers remained cold. From the 'nineties onwards, direct steam heating from the locomotive boiler, through a reducing valve, came into general use, though the flat tin footwarmer died hard on secondary services, and lasted longer still on the once-popular slip carriages. The early corridor trains just described were among the first to provide low-pressure steam heating.

The old pot-lamps, burning rape oil, were abominable things, and provided little light even when, as on the Great Western, two were provided in each compartment. The burner was of the most primitive type and could not be regulated once it was alight. If the wick was too high, it smoked atrociously; yet, with the motion of the carriage, it tended to shake down in its narrow holder and go out. The only attractive thing about the pot lamp was the spectacle of its installation. It was a two-man job. One went along the platform with a barrowload of the lamps, already lighted, in racks. His colleague walked along the roof of the train. At each compartment, they would stop, the man on the roof would pull the wooden plug out of the lamp-hole, the man on the platform would toss up a lighted lamp, which was instantly caught and dropped into place. The operation was extraordinarily quick and beautifully dextrous.

Oil-gas lighting originated with the system introduced in Prussia by Julius Pintsch, and appeared in England on the St. John's Wood branch of the Metropolitan Railway in 1876. The Great Eastern Railway took it up two years later, and thereafter this, and the somewhat similar arrangement of Pope, came into widespread use. The pressure at burner was 84 lb. per sq. in. and the gas was carried between the frames in cylindrical reservoirs which contained, when fully charged, a 40 hour supply. Trouble over the discharge of waste from the Pintsch gas plant at Stratford, Great Eastern Railway, resulted in James Holden adopting it as a locomotive fuel during the 'nineties and nineteen hundreds, this being the first large-scale use of liquid fuel for motive power purposes on a British railway.

As already recorded, the first use of electricity for train lighting, on any railway in the world, took place under Stroudley on the London, Brighton and South Coast in 1881. In October the drawing-room car *Beatrice* was equipped with a 32-cell Fauré battery and twelve Swan lamps. Two months later a four-car Pullman train was similarly equipped. A much better arrangement, of Stroudley's own devising, appeared in 1883, using a belt-driven generator in the van, with accumulators. Elsewhere, the North British Railway in 1882 and the London and North Western in 1884 experimented with steam-driven generators mounted on the locomotive, but for a decade Stroudley's was easily the best arrangement. The modern system, with a small generator under each coach, charging accumulators, was originated by J. Stone in 1894 (single battery) and 1896 (double battery). Oil gas died hard. The Welsbach incandescent mantle gave it new life and new light, more brilliant than that of the early electrical installations. Improvements in the latter, coupled with several serious fires following accidents to gaslit trains, brought gas into increasing disfavour, but it has not vanished yet from old carriages on the northern lines, nor yet from the Great Western. Smaller railways were the first to go in for electric light exclusively, for example, the Great Northern of Ireland; London, Chatham and Dover; London, Tilbury and Southend; and North Stafford.

In the 'nineties, the best main-line stock was noteworthy for its elaborate construction and decoration. Dining- and sleeping-cars built at Wolverton Works by the London and North Western were conspicuous with the most ornate brass handrail arrangements at their end entrances. Saloon carriages for the various royal trains were often flamboyant in style, but in this there was nothing new. As the nineteen-hundreds advanced, there was a strong reaction, particularly marked in the case of the East Coast Joint Stock. Woven wire seats, some of them abominably uncomfortable, but recognized as much more hygenic than the old buttoned-in cushions, enjoyed an increasing vogue. Except on the Midland Railway, the clerestory was used less and less in new stock. When well-designed, its appearance was admirable and its qualities in ventilation and daytime lighting was undoubted. On the other hand it was a complicated arrangement, and keeping it clean was a problem, for which reason many railways, including the North Western, employed it only for dining, sleeping and saloon carriages, whereon it could be given special attention.

End entrances, instead of side doors, began to be used on long-distance ordinary coaches, as well as on Pullmans, diners and sleepers, and some of the finest examples of the end-door coach built during this period were those introduced by the North-Western in 1907 for the American boat specials, and for the famous 2.0 p.m. Scotch expresses. After many vicissitudes, the stock of the Pullman company finally changed hands and came under the exclusive control of an all-British concern, the Pullman Car Company. In 1908 this undertaking placed in service on the London, Brighton and South Coast Railway the first Pullman cars proper to be built as such in Great Britain, forming the celebrated *Southern Belle,* successor to the old Brighton Pullman Limited trains. In 1910 two Pullman buffet cars appeared on the extension line trains of the Metropolitan Railway, a veritable godsend to various old bar-proppers who could now drink their way happily home on the midnight train from Baker Street after other places had closed. The buffet car, however, was considerably older than this; the first train bars, complete with handsome pictures of the highest saloon-lounge standard, had made their appearance on the Great Central Railway when that line opened its London extension. In 1914 the Pullman car re-established itself in Scotland, where it had not been seen since the withdrawal of the Highland sleepers *Balmoral* and *Dunrobin* in 1907. The new cars, employed on the Caledonian and on the Highland Railway south of Aviemore, included dining cars catering for both first- and third-class passengers, and for the beautiful Callander and Oban line, a very handsome Pullman observation car called *Maid of Morven.*

An interesting mechanical innovation in carriage design was Gresley's articulated arrangement, whereby adjacent coach bodies rested on a single bogie. It was first applied in 1907, in the course of re-building old six-wheel and non-bogie eight-wheel coaches, but was later very extensively employed on all kinds of new vehicles. Also in 1907 a very fine pair of royal saloons was built, one by the Great Northern and the other by the North Eastern, in which the first use was made of electric cooking on a British train. Cooking, however, was not exclusively by electricity. Indirect heating combined with ventilation was another interesting feature, anticipating in a simple form the much more elaborate air-conditioning of modern times.

With these fine vehicles we must leave our sketch of railway carriage development during the most interesting phase of its past history, a phase beginning with Clayton's great revolution in carriage design on the Midland Railway, and ending with the 1914 Flying Scotsman, Pullman vestibuled, buckeye-coupled, and altogether quite a familiar-looking East Coast express even to the eyes of to-day.

# CHAPTER EIGHT

# RACING DAYS

AN historical student of locomotives and carriages, translated to the middle 'seventies, would be delighted with the variety and antiquity of much that he would find. But the appraiser of locomotive performance would be largely disappointed. In 1874 the companies responsible for the East Coast and West Coast Routes to Scotland were quite mediocre in this respect. The London and North Western Scotch expresses rumbled northwards at a sort of jog-trot, taking no advantage of the magnificent main line through the level middle of England; they plodded solemnly over Shap and skated down the other side amid the blue smoke and tindery smell of smouldering wooden brake blocks. The Caledonian took over at Carlisle and somehow managed to drag the trains over Beattock and Cobbinshaw, though how Ben Conner's little eight-foot singles ever made the summits without sticking passes comprehension.

On the East Coast Route, there was the same sedate progress; Patrick Stirling's Great Northern engines with their huge driving wheels loped up to Doncaster and York. Beyond that there was the North Eastern, still an indolent, old-fashioned railway with elastic views on punctuality, and beyond that again lay the North British, cleft by an unbridged Firth of Forth, and with, apparently, no notions of timekeeping whatever. Yet, as already remarked, it was that same North British which, with the opening of the new Midland Route in 1876, proceeded to do some of the best locomotive work in the world over one of the most difficult roads in Great Britain. Yet that did not disturb the serenity of the older-established services on either side. The hierarchy of Euston and Kings Cross, whereof the latter had, over twenty years before, turned down Archie Sturrock's constructive plan for an eight-hour run to Edinburgh, knew that with their more direct and more easy routes they were still safe. North British running on the Waverley Route from Edinburgh to Carlisle was an exhibition, but not a menace.

Back in 1874, at any rate, things were really more exciting in the South of England. Even the South Eastern and the London Chatham and Dover ran a few quite good trains against one another, and although the Great Western had lost the real old fighting spirit aroused in the 'forties by the Battle of the Gauges, this company and the London and South Western had their lively encounters. Between London and Exeter (this was long before the opening of the Great·Western's Westbury cut-off), the London and South Western had the shorter route, $171\frac{1}{4}$ miles from Waterloo to Queen Street* compared with the 194 miles of the Great Western and the Bristol and Exeter Railways from Paddington to St. Davids. On the other hand, the South Western was by far the more difficult of the two routes, being a continuous switchback west of a point between Byfleet and Woking.

The rival interests had their crack trains, named after celebrated racehorses of days long ago. From Paddington there was the Flying Dutchman, running, of course, on the broad gauge. It was usually hauled by the big eight-foot singles of Gooch's design, though west of Bristol, Pearson's second (1868) series of 4–2–4 express tank engines, with 8 ft. 10 in. driving wheels, was in evidence. These, however, fell under a cloud after one of them, No. 2001, left the road with the up Dutchman near Bourton in 1876, and the Great Western, which had by then taken over the B. and E. rebuilt them as 8 ft. 4–2–2's with separate tenders.

The London and South Western's flyer was called the Beeswing, and left Waterloo at 2.10 p.m. Like so many on the L.S.W.R. it was a portmanteau train; it departed from Waterloo with two engines and divided at Basingstoke. The pilot engine took its half down to Southampton, Dorchester and Weymouth, with no very distinguished running, while the train engine went on with the remainder to the West of England. It was not a heavy train, but the 6 ft. 6 in. or 7 ft. Beattie 2–4–0 locomotives

* Now Exeter Central.

Maryport and Carlisle
4-0 No. 8 and 0-4-2
No. 4 (rebuilt) outside
Carlisle M. and C.
shed

*Locomotive and General
Railway Photographs*]

Train of mixed Furness,
North Western, and
Midland stock, hauled
by Furness 0-6-2 tank
No. 104

*Locomotive and General
Railway Photographs*]

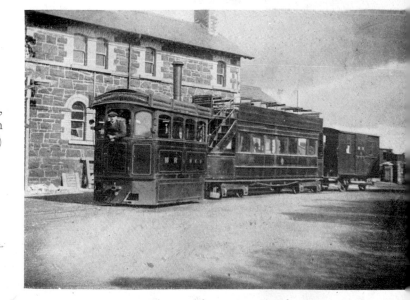

The Portstewart Tram,
Belfast and Northern
Counties (Midland)
Railway

[*K. A. C. R. Nunn*]

The Dandy at [...]
Carlisle, North Bri[...]
Railway. On the d[...]
is painted "For 1st [...]
2nd class passen[...]
only"

[F. Moore's Railway[...]
Photographs]

Douglas train a[...]
Erin, Isle of Ma[...]
way, about [...]
engine Fenella

[F. Moore's [...]
Photograph[...]

Tal-y-llyn Rail[...]
train at Dolg[...]
hauled by Flet[...]
Jennings 0-4-2 [...]
engine. A recent v[...]
taken by the autho[...]

At Markinch, North British Railway, in the 'seventies. Train headed by 2–4–0 locomotive No. 382. The white discs on the buffer beam identified North British trains entering Perth, preventing confusion among Caledonian signalmen.

[*Anthony Murray Collection*]

Skye and the Skye Bogie: Below Ben-na-Caillich, Kyle of Lochalsh, Highland Railway, about 1900.

[*F. Moore's Railway Photographs*]

Between Tregaron and Strata Florida; Manchester and Milford 2-4-0 engine; Great Western vehicles

[*Locomotive and General Railway Photographs*]

Irish-American: Baldwin saddle tank No. 19, entering Cork with up special goods, Cork, Bandon and South Coast Railway, July 25, 1914

[*K. A. C. R. Nunn*]

Lartigue monorail engine, Listowel and Ballybunion Railway, on July 7, 1914

[*K. A. C. R. Nunn*]

Sharp Stewart 0-4-2 engine *Llanerchydol* at Barmouth, Cambrian Railways, about 55 years ago
[*F. Moore's Railway Photographs*]

At Talybont, Brecon and Merthyr Railway; a characteristic Welsh saddle tank piloting a Great Western type B. and M. 2-4-0 tank engine
[*Locomotive and General Railway Photographs*]

Glasgow-Aberdeen express leaving Stirling, Caledonian Railway, hauled by
McIntosh large 4–4–0 No. 140, with "Grampian" 12-wheel coaches
[*F. Moore's Railway Photographs*]

Glasgow and South Western Railway, southbound cattle train passing Rockcliffe,
hauled by Hugh Smellie's large bogie engine, No. 458
[*F. Moore's Railway Photographs*]

North British train climbing to Cowlairs; Holmes 4–4–0 locomotive No. 574,
assisted by cable haulage
[*Locomotive and General Railway Photographs*]

Outside Aberdeen Joint Station: Peter Drummond's Highland Railway engine No. 2, *Ben Alder*, leaving with an Inverness express; on left, a Manson 4–4–0 and semi-corridor six-wheel coach of the Great North of Scotland Railway. The Inverness train, running via Mulben, is also made up of Great North stock

Belfast Express leaving Amiens Street, Dublin, July 20, 1914, hauled by 4–4–0 locomotive No. 173 *Galtee-more*, Great Northern Railway of Ireland

[*K. A. C. R. Nunn*]

Shillelagh–Dublin (Amiens Street) train approaching Bray, Dublin and South Eastern Railway, July 20, 1914, hauled by 4–4–0 engine No. 57 *Rathnew*. The archaic distant signal is noteworthy

[*K. A. C. R. Nunn*]

Down Donaghadee train approaching Neills Hill, Belfast and County Down Railway, hauled by 4–4–2 tank engine No. 30

[*K. A. C. R. Nunn*]

invariably used were, at the same time, scarcely robust, and their work was the more creditable for that. Average speeds were about 42 m.p.h. east of Salisbury and 38 m.p.h. from Salisbury to Yeovil. But thereafter the remaining 48¾ miles to Exeter Queen Street were covered in sixty minutes, including the stop at Exeter ticket platform. From Yeovil to the ticket platform stop, the speed was over 50 m.p.h., and that included the three miles at 1 in 80 from Crewkerne to Hewish summit and the 8½ mile climb to Honiton Tunnel, chiefly at 1 in 70 and 1 in 80. One wonders how on earth the Beattie engines managed to do it, and so well. They had indeed the reputation for being exceptionally free-running engines, except the few that were fitted with piston valves, and the descent from Honiton to Exeter in an old four-wheel second class, at over 70 m.p.h. in places, was more exciting than comfortable.

In spite of names, the real Great Western rival of the Beeswing was not the Flying Dutchman but the Zulu, leaving Paddington at 3.0 p.m. The Dutchman left London at 11.45 a.m., an hour after the South Western's less brilliant morning express to the West. Both the Dutchman and the Zulu made lively starts from Paddington to Swindon, for which run they were allowed 87 minutes, or a start-to-stop average of 53¼ m.p.h. The gradient was gently against the train practically throughout, and the Great Western used heavier stock than the South Western, so the former showed up most favourably against the latter, even allowing for its Basingstoke stop. At Swindon, however, the Great Western was then bound by contract to hold all trains for ten minutes to afford passengers an opportunity for patronising the extremely bad refreshment rooms, and this seemed to discourage all concerned. For while the South Western's timings improved as the Beeswing reached its most westerly and most difficult section, signs of weariness appeared to distinguish Great Western running. Start-to-stop speeds dropped to 47 m.p.h. from Swindon to Bath, and from Bath to Bristol the rate was 44 m.p.h. West of Bristol, the old Bristol and Exeter was inclined to loaf, except coming down Wellington Bank. Certainly, the South Western made the better showing with its climb to Honiton, as compared with the rival interests' climb to Whiteball. These things can scarcely be described as racing, but the two lines, as remarked, exemplified some of the best running in the country during the early 'seventies, and, also as previously noted, both used express engines of decidedly antiquated type compared with those of the northern main lines. Mutual suspicion ran high; without accusing the Great Western of any definitely obstructive tactics, one may record that South Western enginemen passing through Exeter St. Davids on their way to North Devon were made to remember their place by the B. and E. and the Great Western successively; also the latter, while it converted most of the old Bristol and Exeter branches to standard gauge during the years immediately following, left the Chard branch to the very last, for fear the South Western should get running powers over it to Taunton.

In British railway running during the late Victorian period, the fun began on the Anglo-Scottish main lines in 1888. The "racing" started in quite a formal and businesslike way. The standard times between London and Edinburgh were ten hours from Euston and nine from King's Cross. On June 2, the North Western and the Caledonian knocked an hour off their schedule, so that they dead-heated with the East Coast companies, to the latters' great astonishment and annoyance.

The Great Northern was for immediate and open war; the North Eastern reluctant to disturb the peace. The militance of King's Cross prevailed; on July 18 the King's Cross–Waverley time was cut to $8\frac{1}{2}$ hours. This advance of the Great Northern and North Eastern (the North British was a sleeping partner in this business) was short lived. From August 1, the West Coast companies also ran to Edinburgh in $8\frac{1}{2}$ hours. With the material at their disposal, this was a remarkable achievement; for the racing trains the North Western used old Ramsbottom singles of the Problem class, designed as far back as the late 'fifties, as being more free-running engines than the sluggish and erratic three-cylinder compounds and, supposedly, the Jumbo 2–4–0's. The Caledonian employed the celebrated 4–2–2 bogie single

No. 123, built by Neilson and Company for the Edinburgh Exhibition of two years before, and based, apart from the bogie, on Dugald Drummond's North British single-wheelers of 1876, in their turn a modification of Stroudley's *Grosvenor* of 1874 on the London, Brighton and South Coast. On the East Coast lines, the Great Northern used Stirling's eight-foot bogie singles, a design already 18 years old, and the North Eastern employed Tennant 2–4–0's and Worsdell 6 ft. 6 in. 4–4–0 compounds, these last being the only modern engines used, by the standards of the time.

The second dead-heat schedule did not last for long; the North Western was achieving its part by dividing the 10.0 a.m. down express at Preston, whereafter the show part of the train, extremely light in weight, was lifted over Shap as fast as the little engines could manage. From Preston to Carlisle, 105 minutes were allowed for the 90 miles; on the Caledonian, the more difficult stretch of 101 miles from Carlisle to Princes Street was covered in 118 minutes. Two days after the West Coast 8½ hours challenge, the East Coast companies announced an eight-hour timing from King's Cross to Waverley. On August 6, the West Coast did likewise. This was something like racing; the newspapers took up the contest with relish, and there was even an echo in the American press. The drivers were fully alive to the spirit of the thing, and ran ahead of time as far as they dared. Even the pacific powers of the North Eastern were roused, and this company announced on its own that it would cut another quarter-hour from the schedule and bring the train into Waverley at 5.45 p.m. or before.

The *Eighty-eight* suffered, as a contest, from insufficient recording by responsible people. The late Rev. W. J. Scott* managed, however, to travel from King's Cross to York on August 31, the last day of real racing, when two Stirling eight-footers ran from King's Cross to Grantham (just under 105½ miles) and from Grantham to York (82¾ miles) respectively, in 110 minutes and 86 minutes. This was in spite of several

* "Some 'Racing Runs' and Trial Trips," the *Railway Magazine*, July 1897, vol. 1, No. 1.

severe checks north of Grantham, including a maddening one at Selby, where a bargeload of hay was required to pass through the swing bridge opening, and "got the road." On a previous occasion, the King's Cross–Grantham run had been made just about in even time; Mr. Scott believed that it was nearer 106 minutes than the 105 claimed by the officials.

North of York, according to the fallible guards' journals, the 205 miles to Edinburgh were covered in less than 3 hours 39 minutes, including a signal check to a dead stand for nearly two minutes at Ferryhill and a 4¾ minutes stop at Newcastle. On the southern section, a Tennant 2–4–0 was the engine, and a Worsdell bogie compound came on for the Newcastle–Edinburgh run, including its climb from the Border to Grant's-House. Throughout the journey from London, excluding stops, the speed came to just under 60 m.p.h. Thereafter, somebody seems to have had a fright, and the organized if unofficial racing came to an end. But it had served its purpose. The new schedule, to which the companies settled down, was 8 hours 30 minutes between London and Edinburgh, and so it remained for seven years.

The Caledonian Railway, however, once roused, and untroubled by intermediate passenger stops between Carlisle and Edinburgh, continued to make the run in considerably less than scheduled time, using the big single engine No. 123. On one occasion, with about 168 tons behind the tender, this engine made the journey of 100¾ miles at a start-to-stop average of approximately 59 m.p.h., including the 10-mile climb from Beattock to the Summit box at 1 in 88-69, with a pass-to-pass speed of 42.7 m.p.h. and a minimum speed, at the top of the climb, of 38 m.p.h. Thereafter there was the second summit to be crossed at Cobbinshaw, and altogether there were 34 miles of gradient against the engine.

Racing broke out between East and West Coast in the late summer of 1895, but this time from London to Aberdeen, the opening of the Forth Bridge, in 1890, having put the North British Railway in the running for such competition. The last section of the course, from Kinnaber Junction, near Montrose, belonged to the Caledonian, and over it the North British exercised running powers, so whoever reached Kinnaber first had the race in his pocket.

Up to June of 1895, the fastest of the night Scotch expresses was the East Coast train running from King's Cross to Aberdeen, 523½ miles, in 11 hours 35 minutes. By the West Coast Route, the distance was 539¾ miles. It was not only longer; it included the Shap and Beattock climbs. On the other hand, the North British section of the East Coast Route was extremely difficult for fast running, whereas the Caledonian had a fine approach to the critical junction of Kinnaber and was altogether a more promising line once the industrial area was left behind. In that month of June, the West Coast companies announced that their best train would make the complete run from Euston to Aberdeen in 11 hours 40 minutes, only five minutes longer than the East Coast.

This was getting dangerously near dead-heating. The East Coast companies cut their time down to 11 hours 20 minutes, which was considered satisfactory until the West Coast train ran into Aberdeen one morning 11 hours after leaving Euston. So the East Coast train had 35 minutes cut off its time. So far, be it observed, the East Coast was proceeding by the strict rule of timetable running. The companies might knock chunks off the schedules, but they were not yet racing. The West Coast companies had, however, decided that they were doing this very thing. They dropped the timetables, treated their train as an extra-special special, and reached Aberdeen Joint Station 9 hours 59 minutes after leaving Euston.

King's Cross was flabbergasted, for this was not cricket. Indeed, it was not recognized that West Coast had bettered East Coast, for schedules were schedules. On August 14, Patrick Stirling of the Great Northern wrote to his lieutenant F. Rouse at Peterborough: "The L. & N. W. Co. have expressed their intention to reach Aberdeen before us. This of course we cannot permit and arrangements are being made by this Company and the N.E. and N.B. Railways to accelerate the speed of the above train (the 8.0 p.m. from King's Cross) commencing on

Monday next. We must reach York at 11.15 p.m. The load will not exceed six [coaches] whenever possible to keep it to that number and seven will be the maximum in every case. The N.E. Company have undertaken to run their share of the distance at high speed, over $60\frac{1}{2}$ miles per hour York to Newcastle and the N.B. also. Please put your men on their mettle!"

The Great Northern did well, and on the Grantham–York section Stirling eight-footer No. 775 with Driver Lamb up, covered the 82·7 miles in 80 minutes. The load was two vans, three coaches and a sleeping car, equivalent to "$6\frac{1}{2}$ coaches" by the old reckoning. But conventional railway correctitude, not to mention some blunders, got in the way. On the North Eastern, the train lost a full five minutes at Eryholme through signals; even so it reached Edinburgh six minutes ahead of time. Worse happened on the North British. The Scottish drivers were willing, but at Edinburgh Waverley and again at Dundee Tay Bridge, the stationmasters refused to allow any departure before scheduled time. The perpetual unadmitted feud between Locomotive Department and Traffic was still doing its dreary work, and the West Coast came in an easy first at Aberdeen.

On the night of August 20–21, by special instructions from the East Coast Allied High Command, there were no delays whatever to the racing train. East Coast and West Coast trains raced northwards from King's Cross and from Euston. And hours later they approached Kinnaber together. As he pounded up from Montrose, the North British driver saw, far away, the white exhaust of the Caledonian express streaming in the early morning air. The length of the block sections south of Kinnaber favoured the Caledonian, and the junction signalman accepted the latter's train less than 60 seconds before he was offered the North British. The East Coast racer was brought to a stand while the West Coast roared through the junction ahead of it.

On the following night, August 21–22, the East Coast cut a dash indeed. Even allowing for the very light load, the running throughout was magnificent. From King's Cross to Grantham, Driver Falkinder covered the 105·5 miles in 102 minutes with eight-footer No. 668. The second lap carried on the good work, and north of York, Wilson Worsdell's 7 ft. 4–4–0 engines gave splendid running. Of these, No. 1621 ran to Newcastle in 1 hour 20 minutes and No. 1620 (Driver Nicholson) covered the 124·4 miles thence to Edinburgh in 115 minutes. (This last was Charles Rous-Marten's figure; old records at York Museum gave 112 minutes as the time; more evidence of the lack of accurate timing. The highest pass-to-pass speed was 77·1 m.p.h. from Drem to Longniddry Junction, and the final three miles from Portobello into Edinburgh were covered at 60 m.p.h. pass-to-stop.

The North British engines, as already remarked, were faced with a much more difficult job in view of the slacks over the Forth and Tay Bridges, with their severe following curves through Inverkeithing and Dundee Esplanade respectively, and north of Arbroath the line was hilly, tortuous, and partly single-track. One stop only was made, at Dundee, and on most nights of the race the same engine ran through from Edinburgh to Aberdeen. On that early morning of August 22, the North British brought their train to its goal at 4.40 a.m., nearly a quarter of an hour ahead of the Caledonian. The three companies between them had covered the 523 miles from King's Cross in 8 hours 40 minutes, or three minutes under even time including stops. North British speeds were 60·25 m.p.h. Edinburgh to Dundee, and 56·25 m.p.h. Dundee to Aberdeen, with one of Matthew Holmes's 6 ft. 6 in. 4–4–0 locomotives.

The West Coast companies had the last word, though their run of August 22–23 was officially qualified as "exhibition" and only three eight-wheel coaches weighing little more than 20 tons each made a featherweight load behind the tender. Out of Euston the 7 ft. Webb compound *Adriatic* ran to Crewe at a very high average speed—147·5 minutes for the 158·1 miles according to the late C. J. Bowen Cooke. This seems improbable, even for this, the best of the Webb three-cylinder compound classes, but *Adriatic* undoubtedly made a very excellent showing. At Crewe the famous little Jumbo 2–4–0, *Hardwicke*, came on, with Driver Ben Robinson, and covered the

141 miles to Carlisle, with the climb over Shap, at a start-to-stop average of 67·2 m.p.h. North of the Border, the Caledonian threw all conventions overboard, running from Carlisle to Aberdeen with one stop only, at Perth. As a result, Aberdeen, 540 miles from Euston, was reached in 512 minutes. The Caledonian section, 240 miles, was covered in 242 minutes including the stop for changing engines. On the southern section, Drummond 4–4–0 No. 90 covered the 150¾ miles in 149½ minutes, and north of Perth No. 17, one of Lambie's almost identical engines, made the 89¾ miles in 80½ minutes, thus repeating *Hardwicke's* average of 67·2 m.p.h.

It is interesting to notice that while the English companies used locomotives of greatly varied types—Webb compounds and Jumbos on the West, and Stirling singles and Worsdell large four-coupleds on the East Coast, both Scottish companies employed 6 ft. 6 in. 4–4–0 engines of the classic Drummond type, stemming from the old North British design of 1876. Although the most spectacular work in the 'ninety-five races came at the end, when schedules, loads, and doubtless a number of indignant passengers, were left to look after themselves, some of the most creditable running occurred when these things were still held to be of some account. Some very interesting details were published by Rous-Marten in *The Engineer* during the month of the race. On the Caledonian, two Drummond 4–4–0's, Nos. 78 and 90, with 207 tons, ran from Carlisle to Beattock (pass) at 62·37 m.p.h. and thence to a stop at the summit at 41·2 m.p.h. Here No. 78 came off and No. 90 ran to Carstairs (pass) at 62·46 m.p.h., thence to Stirling (stop) at 56·13, giving an average from Carlisle to Stirling of 56·18 m.p.h. including the Summit stop. Engine No. 90 went forward to Perth, making a start-to-stop average of 52·7 m.p.h., after which she was replaced by the Lambie engine No. 17, and the load reduced to 110 tons. Start-to-stop speeds were 58·77 m.p.h., Perth to Forfar, and 58·65 m.p.h. Forfar to Aberdeen ticket platform.

The West Coast "exhibition run" previously mentioned concluded the full-blooded racing of 1895, but enthusiasts hoped for more excitement in the following year, when J. F. McIntosh brought out the first of his famous Dunalastair class engines with the much bigger boiler. But a very unfortunate thing happened on the London and North Western, which alarmed both the company and an influential section of the general public. On the night of July 13, 1896, the down Euston to Aberdeen night express, hauled by two Jumbos, left the road on the sharp curve at Preston. The engines rushed into the adjoining yard, the sleeping cars were thrown about all over the place, and the ordinary composite coach had one end punched in, killing a solitary passenger who was asleep in it.

Now it was no good reading to the world at large a learned lecture on rigid wheelbases and their behaviour at high speeds on sharp curves subject to restriction. The Preston accident was an excessive-speed accident, and high speeds became immediately unpopular, so that much of the good work done by the racing of the previous year came to nothing.

North of the Border, the two Scottish companies continued, however, to show some very lively running indeed. To the North British quarrel with the North Eastern, over the latter's running powers into Edinburgh, I have already referred. While the North Eastern was totally evicted, during 1897–98, no allowance was made for the extra engine stop at Berwick, and start-to-stop speeds of a fraction under 60 m.p.h., including the climb over Grant's-House, were common. The engines usually employed were the same as those which had made such a good showing in the 'ninety-five race, Matthew Holmes's 6 ft. 6 in. 4–4–0's of 1891. An excellent run was made, however, by two of Holmes's seven-footers of 1886, Nos. 598 and 603, with 185 tons and a strong headwind. The 57½ miles were covered in 58 minutes 22 seconds, start-to-stop, and the 11-mile climb from Dunbar to Grant's-House, culminating in the Cockburnspath bank of 1 in 96, was made in the astonishing time of 11 minutes 48 seconds.

For years after the races, too, the Caledonian Railway was distinguished by some of the finest running in the world, on both regular and special occasions. There were the 32-minutes bookings

start-to-stop, for the 32½ miles between Forfar and Perth—
an easy road, it was true—and the 37-minutes schedule for the
much more up-and-down 33 miles from Perth to Stirling. As
for special runs, on February 17, 1906, a football special ran
from Coatbridge to Dundee, 77·6 miles, in 74 minutes. The
load was of five bogies, about 140 tons, and the engine was
McIntosh 4–4–0, No. 902 (Driver Ranochan). An admirable
feature of Caledonian running was the quality of the uphill work.
Very high maxima were unusual, without counterpart to the
London and North Western practice of toiling up one side of
Shap and reeling down the other with the speed rising into the
eighties.

During the first decade of the present century, there arose
intense competition in the South of England, once again
between the Great Western and the London and South
Western, and the object of that competition was transatlantic
traffic between Plymouth and London. The Great Western took
the mails, but a certain number of American passengers used to
leave the steamers at Plymouth. These the South Western used
to lure with siren calls about the shortest route to London,
and with the offer of somewhat old but luxurious central-
corridor coaches (the "American Eagle Express" stock, rebuilt
with bellows connections and coupled up to composite kitchen-
brake-vans). At the beginning of the century, the Great Western
still had to take its West of England passengers up to Bristol
on their way to town, while the South Western took full
advantage of its more direct line, running the boat specials up to
Waterloo with an engine-stop at Templecombe.

The result was not so much racing, as demonstration and
counter-demonstration. There were sinister but quite absurd
stories of American millionaires promising fantastic largesse to
drivers to get them in at such a time. The most spectacular
run of all, made by the Great Western on May 9, 1904, and
timed by Charles Rous-Marten, involved one of the mail
trains, carrying no passengers.

From Plymouth the locomotive was 4–4–0 *City of Truro*,
of the same general type as Dean's Atbaras, with double

frames and outside cranks, but with G. J. Churchward's characteristic taper boiler. The Cities were already known as good runners; in July, 1903, *City of Bath* had worked a royal train from Paddington to Plymouth without a stop, covering the 246⅝ miles in 233½ minutes. *City of Truro*, on the mail train, ran from Plymouth North Road to Exeter St. Davids, 52 miles in 56 minutes, and thence to Bristol (Pylle Hill), 75¼ miles, in 64¼ minutes. Going down Wellington Bank, Driver Clements let his engine rip, and would have done more but for some permanent-way men who were slow in getting out of the way. As it was, Mr. Rous-Marten recorded a briefly maintained maximum of 102·3 m.p.h. At Pylle Hill the load was reduced from five to four mail vans, and *City of Truro* was replaced by *Duke of Connaught*, one of William Dean's 7 ft. 8½ in. singles. This engine ran to Swindon, 46¼ miles, in 39½ minutes, and thence to Paddington, 77¼ miles, in 60 minutes 9 seconds.

The above run furnished a British speed record for many years, and although the maximum on Wellington Bank was eventually dissected and rejected by Cecil J. Allen, on the grounds that the recording instruments employed by Rous-Marten were inadequate and capable of resulting in considerable error over so short a distance, it retains the peculiar indestructibility of anything that has once succeeded in becoming a tradition. The essence of Mr. Allen's very masterly examination was that the 102·3 m.p.h. maximum was not proven and improbable. Needless to say, it is still officially recognized by all Great Western men, whose verdict might be described as "not disproven."

A curious thing is that at the time Rous-Marten would not publish his recording of this speed, on the grounds that it might alarm the public and thus displease the Great Western, and it came to light only after his death, which took place in 1908. Driver Clements, it may be added, lived to the ripe age of 81, and died as recently as 1934. He was the father of three Great Western drivers. Proof and disproof apart, there is no doubt that both locomotives made very fine running indeed, and although Swindon to Paddington is one of the easiest speeding grounds in the world—slightly downhill, with no suburban congestion and with the prevailing winds in rear—a start-to-stop average of just under $77\frac{1}{4}$ miles an hour was good going. The average of a fraction over 70 m.p.h. from Pylle Hill to Swindon, on an undulating course with some relatively severe curvature, was magnificent. *City of Truro's* averages, west of Bristol, were 55·71 m.p.h. Plymouth to Exeter, with its severe gradients and slacks, and 70·27 m.p.h. Exeter to Bristol, including, of course, the climb over Whiteball.

As previously hinted, although the London and South Western had still, at this time, a considerably shorter route than the Great Western, it had also a main line which forbade speeds rising towards even debatable hundreds. Dugald Drummond once considered laying down water troughs, but the only possible level stretch was near Gillingham, Dorset. Nevertheless, South Western enginemen, using the fine Drummond 4–4–0 express engines with bogie tenders, managed to do very remarkable work on this most unpromising road, and in spite of the Great Western's ownership of the short but important link between Cowley Bridge Junction and Exeter St. Davids.

The American boat expresses ran usually at night, and the relatively low volume of goods traffic on the London and South Western, coupled with a complete absence of normal daytime congestion in the London suburban area, gave them a clear road once Exeter was left behind. From the engine-stop at Templecombe to Waterloo, 115 min. was allowed for the $112\frac{1}{4}$ miles. Through Salisbury, which was passed without stopping, there was a very severe slack in force over the reverse curves at the London end of the station. Between the ends of the main-line platforms and the Fisherton Street underbridge the trains had to negotiate a curve of $7\frac{1}{2}$ chains radius leading into one of 10 chains radius. Over this the maximum safe speed was reckoned at 30 m.p.h., and non-stopping trains were supposed to take the curve at less than that. There is no doubt that a number of drivers, if they did not ignore the slack, at least took a very easy view of it. Mr. Rous-Marten, timing one of the up South Western specials on April 23, 1904, with class

T 9 4–4–0 locomotive No. 336, recorded a speed of 75 m.p.h. at the last quarter-mile post preceding the curve and estimated the speed round the curve at 60 m.p.h. The T 9's were undoubtedly very steady and easy-running engines, but this was extremely reckless if Rous-Marten's estimate were correct.

Complaints of excessive speed through Salisbury reached the locomotive department, and Dugald Drummond, whose displeasure was something to be deeply feared, issued "peremptory instructions" to the drivers of the boat trains that they were on no account whatever to run ahead of schedule. For rather more than two years all went well.

On July 1, 1906, the opening of the Great Western Castle Cary-Langport line completed what now became that company's direct route to the West of England, considerably shortening the distance between Paddington, Taunton, and all stations beyond. The Great Western route from London to Plymouth North Road was now 225¾ miles long via Westbury instead of 246¾ via Bristol, and compared with 230¾ on the London and South Western Railway.

Also on July 1st, the up American boat special from Devonport to Waterloo met with the worst accident that ever occurred on the London and South Western, previously a distinctly fortunate line. On the evening of June 30th, 43 passengers had landed at Plymouth off the liner *New York*, and left the same night for Waterloo. The train, consisting of three of the old "Eagle" corridor carriages and the usual kitchen-brake in the rear, kept good time over the 950 ft. summit-level between Bridestowe and Meldon Junction, for it was a light load behind the tender and apparently there was no need for making up time on the easy stretch down from Okehampton to Yeoford. The engine-stop at Templecombe was made punctually, and here the Plymouth engine came off and No. 421, one of Drummond's nearly new large-boilered 6 ft. 7 in. 4–4–0's, came on. At 1.57 a.m. the train ran through Salisbury at very high speed. Exactly what happened is uncertain, for it was quite dark and the few people on the station had their views variously obstructed. An old Beyer Peacock goods engine was standing in the Bournemouth bay, and between it and the express a down milk-empties train was coming slowly into the station. It would appear that No. 421 rolled badly on entering the curve at full speed, and although she negotiated the $7\frac{1}{2}$-chain radius, her nearside wheels lifted clear of the rails on the slightly easier curve following. Derailment did not take place in the usual sense of the term, but the express engine, as she heeled over to the right on the left-hand curve, fouled the vans of the empty milk train, tipped right over and tended to fly off at a tangent, being brought up by the old goods on the farthest track. The tender shut up on the engine, jacknife fashion, and the three coaches were thrown in all directions; bodies and frames parted company and the former were smashed to pieces against one another, against the overturned tender, and on the girders of the Fisherton Street Bridge. The Bournemouth platform kept the goods engine upright and prevented all but a few smaller pieces of wreckage from falling into the street on that side. Of the express vehicles, only the rear van escaped destruction. Twenty-four passengers, over half the entire company, both the enginemen on No. 421, the guard of the milk train and the fireman of the goods engine, lost their lives. No explanation was therefore to be had as to why the experienced driver of No. 421 entered the curve at such a speed; both men on the engine were caught between tender and backplate, were killed instantly, and resembled nothing human. One may speculate, though no more, on the fact that this wild run from Templecombe coincided to the day with the opening of the Great Western cut-off, and on what irresponsible minor officers may or may not have said previously to the driver of No. 421 regarding this outflanking move by the enemy. Also, it is possible that the driver might have done what he did with impunity on one of the smaller, older engines. No. 336, previously mentioned, had the boiler pitched nine inches lower than that of No. 421, and calculations made afterwards suggested that to overturn the latter a speed of 67 m.p.h. would have been necessary round the curve.

Rivalry between the two companies continued for a while,

though it was now a frightened and correspondingly decorous rivalry. Two years after the accident, the South Western tried to charm the transatlantic passengers with superior amenities; if they could no longer be raced up to town in time to go to bed in a London hotel, they might sleep peacefully from Plymouth to Waterloo and lie abed at the latter till breakfast time. Four very fine sleeping-cars, with brass beds instead of berths, were put on. But two years later again, the South Western sold these to the Great Western, which very soon lost two of them in a paint-shop fire at Swindon. The two companies settled down to the safe and unexciting respectability of a working agreement, and the old fighting days, dating from the South Western's first access to Exeter in 1860, were over.

The Salisbury accident did damage, in popular reactions, to the cause of high speed, however well-conducted, as the Preston smash had done before it. To make matters worse, there were in 1906 and 1907 two more inexplicable derailments at high speed, at Grantham on the Great Northern and Shrewsbury on the London and North Western. In each case, as at Salisbury, the enginemen on the derailed trains were killed outright. At Grantham, on September 19th, the offending train ran through signals, failing to make its booked stop there, and was derailed on a crossover. On a previous occasion the driver had complained of illness while on duty. At Shrewsbury there was no slowing down for the station stop, the engine went over as before, and Lieut.-Colonel Yorke, who conducted the inquiry, considered that the driver was probably asleep on the footplate, and that his mate was either unaware of this or also asleep.

This series of accidents, beginning and ending a period of eleven years, formed a sad complement to the finest outburst of competitive running since the days of the Battle of the Gauges, when the Great Western had done the most remarkable things with the old Gooch singles. Preston, Salisbury, Grantham and Shrewsbury presented no case against fast running, only against reckless running, which is a very different thing. But there were no more races, or anything resembling races, and though there were many good trains running in the summer of 1914 the excitement had gone, not to return until the nineteen-thirties when the railway companies at last woke up to the fact that they were being threatened, not by other railway companies, but by the internal combustion engine, the rubber tyre and the open road.

Featherweight Express: S. W. Johnson's single No. 1853 with a Manchester Dining-Car train (carriages of the final Clayton design); in the background is one of F. W. Webb's four-cylinder compound eight-coupled coal engines for the London and North Western Railway

# CHAPTER NINE

# BYWAYS AND ODDITIES

A FEW weeks before writing this, I was saddened by a dreary little notice in one of the papers to the effect that the Festiniog Railway had closed down. It was a vague, unsatisfactory notice, for it did not even give a definite statement that the closure was final, or that the line might be reopened sometime. It seemed that this railway, the most interesting, and in some ways the most important small narrow-gauge railway in the world, was simply fading out, and that nobody knew whether this was for ever, or cared. One of the Festiniog's principal claims to general interest was that it was the oldest small-gauge railway in the world,* for it was opened, with horse traffic, on April 20, 1836. The Nantlle Railway, also in North Wales, was older, having been opened in 1828, on the 3 ft. 6 in. gauge, but this did not survive as a narrow-gauge railway for over a century, as did the Festiniog, with its gauge of 1 ft. 11½ in. For a very full and learned history of these, and of the other narrow-gauge lines in North Wales, the reader is recommended to consult Charles E. Lee's *Narrow-Gauge Railways in North Wales* (Railway Publishing Co., 1945).

The Festiniog's most important claim was that it was the first steam small-gauge railway, locomotives having been introduced in the summer of 1863. Passenger traffic began unofficially in the following year, and officially, with Government approval, in the beginning of 1865. As a steam passenger line, the Festiniog Railway was a model for light and mountain railways all over the world. The original locomotives were George England's 0–4–0 outside-cylinder tanks, with auxiliary tenders, but in 1869 there appeared *Little Wonder*, a Fairlie's patent double-bogie double-boiler engine, of the type that the

* As opposed to narrow gauge; the four-foot gauge, for example, was older than this.

Festiniog was to employ for all its heaviest traffic in the uphill direction (the slate trains came down by gravity) for the rest of its active existence. No other British railway employed the Fairlie engine for any length of time, though it enjoyed some popularity abroad and several series of big Fairlies worked for years on the Mexican Railway.

Few small railways could compare with the Festiniog for the great beauty and variety of the country they traversed, and that is judgment by worldwide standards. There was a real thrill in traversing, and not only for the first time, its dizzy ways above the mountain treetops about Tan-y-Bwlch; its tunnel, fitting the train like finger of glove, provided a delightfully infernal experience in travelling, and the results of a window left open going through it towards Blaenau Festiniog could lay you out. There was a tremendous swank about those little trains, too. You could make your first acquaintance with the line at Minffordd Junction, and your progress hitherto, by the Cambrian Railways from Barmouth, might well have had an unhurried, bucolic character. But the little Festiniog train with its double engine and its low-down bogie carriages would come spanking in on the high level with all the air—and the particular noise—of a great express making a call by the way. The railway had all the qualities of greatness in miniature, like certain kinds of scenery; acquaintance with the Matterhorn cannot take away the majesty of Sgurr nan Gillean, or the little vastitude of the Langdale Valley; bright Venus outshines Jupiter's huge planet.

Quite otherwise was the Tal-y-Llyn Railway, farther south down Cardigan Bay. Here, truly, was a railway like an Emett drawing come to life, with its little ancient tank engines, its bumping toy carriages and its primitive systems of water supply for locomotive purposes. It began operations in 1865 and has not changed since then. Ironically enough, with its equipment dating back over eighty years, and with grass and heather growing between the rails of its 2 ft. 3 in. gauge tracks, the Tal-y-Llyn Railway has, as I write, outlived the much more imposing Festiniog—if the latter is indeed not sleeping but dead. Unlike most of the photographic illustrations to this book, that of the Tal-y-Llyn train at Dolgoch was taken quite recently. Yet, but for the brevity of the skirts disappearing on the right, it might have been taken any time since the 'sixties.

Until the late inter-war years, Wales abounded in narrow-gauge lines in the mountain valleys; there was the North Wales Narrow Gauge system, which enjoyed, though rather briefly, a second and magnified flowering as the Welsh Highland Railway, with physical connection to the Festiniog at Portmadoc. Down by Aberystwyth, the Great Western Railway still happily maintains, purely as a holiday line in the season, the Vale of Rheidol Railway up to Devil's Bridge. Narrow-gauge Welsh railways depending on some great local industry, such as the Padarn Railway down from Dinorwic Quarries to the Menai Strait, are still with us; so are such lines, taken over by the Great Western, as the Corris and the Welshpool and Llanfair, though they no longer carry passengers, officially at any rate.

If only the same could be said for the Southern Railway's ownership of that delectable Lynton and Barnstaple Railway in North Devon, one of the loveliest things of its kind. Not that one should speak too harshly of the Southern for closing it. A deputation of local worthies attended upon the Southern, to show reason why the Lynton and Barnstaple should be kept up, and on inquiry it transpired that the deputation had come, severally but solidly, by car. I enjoyed hearing about the antics of the price of coal in Lynton and Lynmouth after the railway had been abandoned. The L. and B. was one of those small undertakings, the existence of which was enjoyed by sufficient people to justify the writing and publication of a delightful illustrated history (by L. T. Catchpole; Oakwood Press, 1936). The coast of North Devon and Somerset would seem to have been unhealthy for minor railways. There, southwards from Watchet into the Brendon Hills, once ran the West Somerset Mineral Railway, born of Somerset iron ore and killed by cheaper ore from abroad. In this case the railway outlived its own usefulness by many years. It was a standard-gauge line, though it was quite isolated from the rest of the British railway

163

system, and it was opened in 1859, with a relatively level line as far as Combe Row, whence a tremendous cable-worked incline ran up to Brendon Hill. Along the top of the hills it ran westwards to Gupworthy, with a summit level, a little beyond Brendon, of 1,344 ft. above sea level, the second highest railway summit in the South of England.

Now, a funny thing happened in the early days of the railway; the Ebbw Vale Steel, Iron and Coal Company became interested in the Brendon Hill mines, and in 1864 made an agreement to work the railway for 55¼ years. During the 'eighties the bottom fell out of the Somerset ore industry, but the Ebbw Vale Company had to carry on with the railway. At the beginning of 1898 there was one train daily, each way, between Watchet and Combe Row, hauled by the solitary engine, an old Sharp long-boiler saddle tank called *Pontypool*, and the Ebbw Vale Company asked to be relieved of its responsibility. To this the railway company agreed, on condition that the guaranteed annual rent (£5,575) went on being paid for the full term of the agreement.

And so it was. Except for a brief period of operation with an old Metropolitan tank locomotive (No. 37) by the Somerset Mineral Syndicate during 1907–9, no regular trains ran after 1898, but the railway had its annual pot of gold from Ebbw Vale until 1919. There were some odd stories about the transport of the Metropolitan engine to Watchet in 1907. A temporary connection was put in with the Great Western Railway which brought the old thing down from London, but there was a difference in Metropolitan and Great Western clearances, and No. 37 seems to have had her rake-off in respect of water-troughs and other components of the Great Western anatomy. At all events, the Great Western would not accommodate such a destructive engine a second time, and after the line finally closed in 1909, the Metropolitan veteran departed from Watchet by sea.

The earliest minor railways to be known by generations of holidaymaking Londoners were those of the Isle of Wight. The island's railway history was involved, and its oldest line was not the Isle of Wight Railway, but the Cowes and Newport Railway, opened in June, 1862. With other locally promoted lines it became part of the Isle of Wight Central Railway, the largest system in the island, which pursued a hopeful business career, chiefly with second-hand locomotives and rolling stock of ancient and honourable (but especially ancient) extraction. The Freshwater, Yarmouth and Newport Railway was opened in 1888 for goods and in the following year for all traffic, which was worked until 1913 by the Central, for a while with a railmotor and a push-and-pull set, improbably though truly composed of an outside-cylinder 0–4–2 saddle-tank engine with the cab about 18 inches higher than the chimney, coupled to a relatively enormous ex-Midland 12-wheel clerestory carriage, bought in 1907. Then the F.Y.N. evicted its operating company and courageously undertook to work its own line. Somehow, somewhere, there was benevolent support from the Great Central; some old Manchester, Sheffield and Lincolnshire carriages were shipped to the south, an ex-Brighton Stroudley "Terrier" was obtained at third-hand from the London and South Western and a Manning Wardle 0–6–0 saddle tank from somewhere else. With this equipment, the F.Y.N. managed to stay afloat, though bankrupt, while the Central was cheerfully waiting for it to sink.

The Isle of Wight Railway, though smaller than the Central, was somehow much more respectable. Beginning operations in 1864, it lacked the Central's old-junk-shop atmosphere as to locomotives and rolling stock, having bought all but one of its locomotives new from Beyer, Peacock and Co., these being of that firm's standard 2–4–0 tank design with inside frames. Though the class was ancient, it had the dignity of near-uniformity. The carriages, however, included some old stagers of the non-bogie eight-wheel order, second-hand from the Metropolitan, which came to grace the Ryde-Ventnor "expresses" after long years of jogging round the Inner Circle. The first stretch of Vectisian railway to be encountered by most visitors from London belonged to none of the island railways. From Ryde Pierhead to St. John's Road the line was jointly owned by the South Western and the Brighton, who sank their feud thus far, and occupied by the I.W.R. and I.W.C.R. on terms of armed neutrality. The Central had a devil of a job with clearances when it imported its wonderful Midland carriage and hauled it inland over this line; the whole roadbed had to be lowered under one overbridge.

Cornwall had a number of interesting minor railways in the old days, in addition to the Bodmin and Wadebridge, already noticed. There was the Redruth and Chacewater, of 4 ft. gauge and dating back to 1825, with its three ancient locomotives *Miner*, *Smelter* and *Spitfire*. Steam traction had been introduced in 1854, and during our period the original locomotives continued to serve the R. and C.R. for its easygoing mineral traffic. *Miner*, however, was of a type older than the 'fifties, and was probably the last railway engine to run in Great Britain with the Gothic-shaped firebox dome characteristic of Robert Stephenson's practice in the 'thirties and 'forties of last century.

The Light Railways Act of 1896, under which, subject to strict speed restrictions, local railways could be built and run much more cheaply than those built to main-line standards, gave something of a fillip to local railway transport. Even so, several railways of light character had been built, technically as tramways, long before that Act. A favourite with many who had leanings towards the quaint and rural in railway travel was the Wantage Tramway, which might have been described as a tramway for passengers and a railway for goods traffic. For the former were carried in genuine tramcars, hauled, usually, by steam dummy locomotives of the type once common in Midland and Northern manufacturing towns, while goods was conveyed in ordinary wagons by small railway-type 0–4–0 tank engines. Of these last the most famous was undoubtedly *Jane*, originally built by George England in 1857 for Captain Peel's privately sponsored Sandy and Potton Railway and named *Shannon* after the gallant gentleman's ship.

At Wantage, whither she came at the sprightly age of 21, she was always known as *Jane*. She outlasted passenger traffic, with its exorbitant ninepenny fare for a journey of $2\frac{1}{2}$ miles, by many years, becoming the oldest locomotive in public service in Great Britain, and certainly one of the oldest in the world. The Wantage Tramway came to the close of its chequered existence at the end of 1945, but not *Jane*. The Great Western bought her, as an antique treasure, and added to the ancient glories of her immense chimney and classical tea-urn dome a pair of new brass nameplates. So *Jane* has once more become *Shannon*, as when George England built her. Well, well—she has been an old and faithful servant, and when she was young, servants were known by their surnames in the smartest circles.

Southern and Eastern England had several light railways built under the Act of 1896. Still there survives the delicious Kent and East Sussex. It began in 1900 as the Rother Valley, and was to have grown into something quite ambitious, linking Pevensey with the Medway at Maidstone, with branches to Rye, Cranbrook and Appledore. But it never got beyond Headcorn in the north and Robertsbridge in the south: the trees brush its one-coach mixed train, and there are lizards in the grassy yard at Rolvenden.

East Anglia possessed, not only some highly diverting branches of the Great Eastern, but three rich gems in the shape of the Southwold Railway, the Mid-Suffolk Light Railway and the Colne Valley and Halstead Railway. The late lamented Southwold, of 3 ft. gauge, probably had more comic postcards to its address than any other railway in Europe. The M.S.L.R. gave you the pretty and improbable spectacle of red locomotives with brass domes plodding fussily along under the vast cloudscapes of Eastern England. The Colne Valley and Halstead Railway was not of the "light" order, dating back to 1860, and as will be seen from Mr. Nunn's photograph, it had a distinct flavour of the Great Eastern about its trains. But there were some quite un-Great Eastern antiques around at various times. In the last century there was an ancient London, Brighton and South Coast single tank engine with a highly ornamental fluted dome, stemming from the far-off generation of the terrifying John Chester Craven, whose bizarre collection of Brighton locomotives strangely belied the harsh and austere regime behind them. Another most interesting relic was the company's best set of carriages during the present century, which was used until the London and North Eastern took over. It was a neat rake of three bogie coaches, save that there was something distinctly odd about the brake third at one end. This looked as if it had once carried other things besides passengers and luggage. It had. Those three coaches came from the original experimental electric train of the District Railway, which had run an exhibition shuttle service between Earls Court and Kensington High Street in 1900. The Colne Valley's queer looking brake third, which had raised floors at the ends, was the original District motor coach. After the experiments, the carriage was gutted, as a motive unit, and the C.V. and H.R. thriftily acquired the remains, together with two ordinary coaches.

Over on the Welsh Marches there were two very jolly railways, whereof the Shropshire and Montgomeryshire was the most respectable. This line, which still exists for goods traffic, was a Light Railway resurrection of part of the Potteries, Shrewsbury and North Wales Railway, an unhappy undertaking which never succeeded in connecting or even approaching either the Five Towns or North Wales, and fell derelict far back in the Victorian era. The S. and M. was one of the group of local railways which rose to mild fame under the late Colonel H. F. Stephens, who made a business of collecting small or moribund railways and licking them into shape. A Shropshire and Montgomeryshire "express" before the first German war would consist of three old Midland bogie carriages and a four-wheel van, hauled by an ex-London and South Western 0–6–0 of the well-known Ilfracombe class. There were three of them on the S. and M., *Hesperus*, *Pyramus* and *Thisbe*. In addition to these and other units, the S. and M. had one extreme oddity and one historic antique, a locomotive and a coach respectively. The former was called *Gazelle*, and was a miniature standard-gauge 2–2–2 tank engine, later altered to 0–4–2, with wooden wheels. The carriage was originally the Queen's saloon on the

London and South Western, designed by Joseph Beattie and known, by the evidence of an old lithograph, to have been in existence at least as early as 1844. Colonel Stephens used it as an inspection car; he had a similar, but slightly less ancient carriage on the Kent and East Sussex. This had been an admired exhibit in the Crystal Palace in 1851.

The Bishops Castle Railway was not respectable. It had been in Chancery for a few generations, for so long, indeed, that even the Receiver was sensitive about it, and there was a row if people tried to photograph it. But it carried on down the years, with its overgrown tracks drunk with honeysuckle and meadow-sweet, its ancient signals giving various equivocal indications somewhere between "stop" and "clear," its station at Stretford Bridge Junction which was to all intents and purposes without access except by train, and its trains which were ghosts of those that had ranged the British main lines sixty years ago. All sorts of ancient rolling stock found their way to the Bishops Castle Railway; antique locomotives from the Somerset and Dorset and the Great Western; carriages with chain brakes from the London and North Western; other carriages from the South Western and the Hull and Barnsley, but all of a kind that few could remember having used on the parent systems.

It was fitting that the Bishops Castle should have its beginning at Craven Arms on the Shrewsbury and Hereford line. Craven Arms is hard by Stokesay, and just as Stokesay Castle showed you English domestic architecture, complete with all the modern conveniences of the thirteenth century, mellowed and for centuries untouched by the hand of war, so did the Bishops Castle Railway, opened in 1866, preserve British railway practice of the industrial middle ages, likewise overgrown and embowered in the country it had sought to serve. All the station clocks seemed to have stopped between 1890 and 1900, if not earlier; at Bishops Castle station the guard used to listen for the striking of the church clock when he knew it was round about train time. It was a perfect railway for a tranquil holiday; the journey from Craven Arms to Bishops Castle, $10\frac{1}{2}$ miles, occupied 50 minutes.

But at least the Bishops Castle Railway succeeded in connecting its namesake town with the main British railway system, which was the original intention, and this was more than could be said for some British railways. Of such lines we have already noticed, briefly, the Lancashire, Derbyshire and East Coast, and the luckless Potteries, Shrewsbury and North Wales. They were British counterparts of those American railways which wandered out from weatherboard cities in the West to lose themselves in the prairie, while they bravely styled themselves the Something, Somewhere and Pacific Railroad. In Wales there was the Manchester and Milford Railway, which was intended to link Manchester with America via Pembrokeshire and thus, among other things, somewhat to shorten the time taken by cotton to travel from Georgia and the Carolinas to English mills. It was opened in 1866, but it never got nearer to Manchester than Aberystwyth (110 miles away, airline distance), or nearer to Milford Haven than Pencader, about 36 miles, or $53\frac{3}{4}$ miles by Great Western through Carmarthen and Clarbeston Road.

Yet there was the Manchester and Milford Railway, with 40 miles of route, an independent line owning locomotives and rolling stock. One of those locomotives exploded, long years ago, which is why, to this day, there is a considerable chunk of locomotive boiler somewhere in the River Tivy. The line was leased by the Great Western from 1906, and eventually incorporated in that company's system. In contradistinction to the Manchester and Milford, among small railways, was the Wrexham, Mold and Connahs' Quay Railway. Its title was ponderous, but still truly descriptive of where it went. One of its proud possessions, at a time when such things were practically unheard of in Britain, was an 0–8–0 tank engine, a gawky and unkempt-looking saddle tank which had been rebuilt and elongated out of something smaller and altogether more ordinary. The Great Central took it over in 1905.

Scotland had a number of light railways, but of these the only one to work its own system was the Campbeltown and Machrihanish, whose 2 ft. 3 in. gauge line began on the quay at Campbeltown, where the Clyde steamers came in, and crossed the narrow neck of Kintyre to where the Atlantic rollers roared on Machrihanish Bay. With its fussy little olive green 0-6-2 tank engines, *Argyll* and *Atlantic*, and its green-and-white saloon carriages, it was the nearest approach to a Hebridean railway ever built, though at one time there were prospects of narrow-gauge lines being built in Arran, Skye and Lewis.

The Scottish main-line railways operated some of the quaintest lines in Great Britain. In the depth of winter I have sat—and that was in London and North Eastern times—the solitary passenger in the morning train from Fountainhall to Lauder, and wistfully watched the enginemen and guard get off and join the stationmaster at Oxton, who was frying sausages in the office. On the North British branch from Drumburgh Junction to Port Carlisle, before 1913, a single horse-drawn carriage or "dandy" formed the train. It was a gentling experience to watch the branch home signal dropped for this equipage, to see the old brown pony come trotting round into Drumburgh, and to stand him a carrot while you waited for the Carlisle train to roll in from Silloth. He and his stable companions have long gone to Pegasus's bosom, but the old dandy car, on which the third-class passengers sat outside, jaunting car fashion, survives as a museum piece of the L.N.E.R.

The Isle of Man Railway, which began in 1873 with a short line across the island from Douglas to Peel, added a long branch to Port Erin, and took in the formerly independent Manx Northern Railway from St. Johns to Peel, is still one of the most interesting narrow-gauge railways in the British Isles, even though its beautiful little Beyer Peacock tank engines are beginning to lose, at last, their classic brass domes and copper-capped chimneys. Those locomotives have an interesting lineage. In 1866, Beyer, Peacock and Company were required to design an engine suitable for the new 3 ft. 6 in. gauge railways which were beginning to invade the mountain places of Norway. So they produced a miniature version of their standard Metropolitan-type engine of 1864, giving it a two-wheeled instead of a four-wheeled Bissel radial truck. When the I.M.R.

was shortly to begin business, the Norway design was adapted to the 3 ft. gauge, and this remained thereafter the standard Manx locomotive, gradually increasing in size and power from the old *Sutherland* of 1873 to the *Mannin* of 1926.

Small as they are, the Isle of Man locomotives have long shown themselves to be very lively machines indeed, whether working singly on light winter trains, or three together (one behind) on some immensely long summer excursion. They have had their exciting moments too, as when *Tynwald* and *G. H. Wood* met on the single track between Douglas and Port Soderick. I heard the story from the late Mr. David Dow, who used to keep the pub at St. John's, and who explained to me, over the top of his bar, how he had come to have a visible crater in the dome of his forehead. He was driving *Tynwald* northbound from Port Erin and running bunker first when he saw *G. H. Wood* coming up the hill at him. In the unprotected "tin box," no engineman would have stood a chance in such a situation. His fireman went off the engine one side, and he the other, falling down the embankment and acquiring that bash on the head from a stump on the way, while *G. H. Wood* smacked into *Tynwald's* cab and instantly knocked it flat. Driver Dow's railway career was over, though the fault was not his. After a long, slow recovery, the Isle of Man Railway set him up in the pub, a lucrative one at that, where for the rest of his days he would delight the elect, over their beer, with engine-driving stories as racy and exciting as any from the Wild West.

As already remarked, Ireland had many narrow-gauge railways and several broad-gauge ones quite as quaint. Among them was the West Clare, clanking across the heather on its circuitous course from Ennis to Kilrush; there was the Clogher Valley, half railway and half tramway, with its boxed-in locomotives which always ran backwards, clanging their way down the main street of Fivemiletown; there was the Dublin and Blessington Tramway, with its double-deck cars and its locomotives with cabs at both ends. In its day, one of the most imposing of small Irish railways, and also the most extensive

light railway to be built under the Railways (Ireland) Act of
1896, was the Londonderry and Lough Swilly. The original
section, however, from which the company took its name, was
much older, and began its life with the Irish broad gauge.
Under the 1896 Act were built the branch from the old terminus
at Buncrana to Carndonagh, and the wildly wandering, fifty-
mile long Burtonport Extension line, both on the 3 ft. gauge.

Travelling out to Burtonport on the west coast indeed took
you far beyond the Pale; as you rumbled along Owencarrow
Viaduct in the teeth of one of those tremendous westerly gales
that were later to blow a train over at this place, the train
became a smaller and a smaller thing; on a squally winter
evening the country grew more vast and more eerie; you
thought of Dalua in the first act of *The Immortal Hour* crying
of his journey to the abyss beyond the world, and the carriage
wheels might take up the mocking chorus:

> You have come but a little way, who think so far
> The long uncounted leagues to the world's end!

It could be a mental, as well as a physical relief at the end
of your journey to sit drinking bottled Guinness in the friendly,
slatternly coffee-room of an easygoing Irish hotel. For the
Burtonport trains the company used a pair of 4–8–0 tender
locomotives and a 4–8–4 tank engine, the only examples of
these types in the British Isles.

From the grandly awful of such a journey to the remote
north-west, you could turn to the quaint grotesque of the
Waterford and Tramore Railway, a broad-gauge line which
seemed to exist principally by conveying large school-treats,
organized and otherwise. It was one of those incredibly historical
lines, on which you could walk back into the middle of the
previous century simply by taking a ticket and getting on to
a train. At the beginning of this century, it still possessed, and
used, an ancient Bury tank engine with bar frames and a haycock dome. It was built about 1845 and was bought from the
contractor when the W. and T.R. started business in 1853.
This most antique locomotive ran until 1905, and was not
broken up until 1909.

Of the three remaining Tramore engines, two were six-wheel-single well-tanks, of very pretty appearance, built by Fairbairn in 1855, and the other a sprightly youngster of an 0–4–2 tank, by Slaughter, Gruning & Co., built as recently as 1862. The carriages were in keeping with the engines, for they were of the archaic type with the compartments in the form of curved coach bodies; some had the sides open to leeward, though the usual windows were provided on the weather side, and at least one, possibly bought second-hand from the Midland Great Western Railway, had a boot which had once held a folding bed. Sleeping accommodation was not, however, necessary on the Waterford and Tramore Railway, with its isolated main line, 7¼ miles long.

There were many oddities in Ireland; even the dignified Great Northern favoured the Fintona branch with a horse tram, and for that matter still does so. But the Listowel and Ballybunion Railway beat the lot. Opened in 1888, with a line 9¼ miles long, it was a Lartigue monorail, steam-operated, with its single running rail on triangular trestles which rested on the sleepers and bore lower down a pair of guiding rails, to prevent the trains from rolling. The locomotives, built by the Hunslet Engine Company, had three coupled axles and two cylinders, supplied by a pair of ordinary loco-type boilers, mounted one each side. The tenders were also equipped with cylinders and two coupled axles, but, latterly at any rate, this additional complication was kept out of gear. Both passenger carriages and wagons were arranged pannier fashion; travellers sat with their backs to the rail and their feet outwards: horses and cows rode head-first, balancing one another in pairs. To enable passengers to cross through the train at stations, a dummy carriage with a sort of stile on it was marshalled at a strategic point in the line of vehicles.

It was an ingenious, but clumsy kind of railway; points were impossible, movement from one track to another had to be made by means of turntables, and instead of level crossings, wooden draw-bridges of peculiarly Heath Robinsonian character enabled Shawn and Bridie to drive their turf-cart across the railway. Sometimes they forgot to raise the bascules after passage. Yet the Lartigue system of railway transport had its large-scale copyists. The Behr monorail incorporated the same principle of a single raised rail with balanced cars running on it, by electric power in this case, and in 1900 a monorail company actually got the necessary powers to build such a line from Liverpool to Manchester, to the surprise and alarm of the London and North Western and the Cheshire Lines. Parliament, however, was more favourable than the investing public, and the most the Behr system did, like Brennan's gyroscopic monorail, was to excite the imagination of the late H. G. Wells.

That must end our note on oddities, and indeed end our story for the present. Much that should have been described has not been so; electric railways, I know, have had a very poor deal in this book, but my object has been rather to recapture the beauty and the splendour of steam in the great days of its monopoly. Nothing else resembles, or can resemble, the steam railway train. It is still with us, and, for steam is a hardy agent subject to few ailments, it is likely to remain for long, though the locomotives of to-day may not be the clean, carefully tended things that we once knew.

Those were the trains we loved; grand, elegant and full of grace. We knew them, and they belonged to the days when we first gazed on the magic of cloud shadows sweeping over the Downs, when we first became fully aware of the smell of a Wiltshire village after rain, or when we first saw a Scottish mountain framed in a double rainbow so vivid that no painter dare to try to record it; to the days when, unadvised and at random, we discovered and first read Jefferies' *Bevis*. Those were the days when we first looked with the uncomprehending pleasure of early boyhood on a beautiful woman in a flowing Burne-Jonesian dress, when we first heard with awed and incredulous delight the music of Elgar, and they were the days when the steam locomotive, unchallenged, bestrode the world like a friendly giant.

·175

## NOTEWORTHY BRITISH EXPRESS LOCOMOTIVES

### 1874–1914

| Railway | Designer | Date | Type | Cylinders | Driving wheels | Evaporative heating surface | Superheater | Grate area | Pressure |
|---|---|---|---|---|---|---|---|---|---|
| | | | | inches | ft. in. | sq. ft. | sq. ft. | sq. ft. | lb. per sq. in. |
| 1. Highland | D. Jones | 1874 | 4–4–0 | 18 × 24(o) | 6 3 | 1,228 | — | 16¼ | 160 |
| 2. L.N.W.R. | F. W. Webb | 1874 | 2–4–0 | 17 × 24 (i) | 6 7½ | 1,083 | — | 17·1 | 140 |
| 3. N.B.R. | D. Drummond | 1876 | 4–4–0 | 18 × 26 (i) | 6 6 | 1,193 | — | — | 150 |
| 4. Midland | S. W. Johnson | 1877 | 4–4–0 | 18 × 26 (i) | 7 0 | 1,313 | — | 17·5 | 140 |
| 5. G. & S.W.R. | H. Smellie | 1879 | 2–4–0 | 18 × 26 (i) | 6 9½ | 1,206 | — | 16 | 140 |
| 6. N.E.R. | T. W. Worsdell | 1888 | 4–2–2 | {(1) 20 / (1) 28} × 24 (i) | 7 7¼ | 1,139 | — | 20·7 | 175 |
| 7. L.N.W.R. | F. W. Webb | 1889 | 2–2, 2–0 | {(2) 14 / (1) 30} × 24 | 7 1 | 1,242 | — | 20·5 | 175 |
| 8. L.B.S.C. | W. Stroudley | 1889 | 0–4–2 | 18¼ × 26 (i) | 6 6 | 1,485·4 | — | 20·65 | 150 |
| 9. G.N.R. | P. Stirling | 1894 | 4–2–2 | 19½ × 28 (o) | 8 1½ | 1,031·7 | — | 20 | 170 |
| 10. G.W.R. | W. Dean | 1894 | 4–2–2 | 19 × 24 (i) | 7 8½ | 1,561·3 | — | 20·8 | 160 |
| 11. N.E.R. | W. Worsdell | 1896 | 4–4–0 | 20 × 26 (i) | 7 7¼ | 1,216 | — | 20·75 | 175 |
| 12. C.R. | J. F. McIntosh | 1896 | 4–4–0 | 18¼ × 26 (i) | 6 6 | 1,403·2 | — | 20·6 | 160 |
| 13. G. & S.W.R. | J. Manson | 1897 | 4–4–0 | {(2) 12½ × 24 (o) / (2) 14½ × 26 (i)} | 6 9½ | 1,173 | — | 18 | 165 |
| 14. L. & Y. | J. Aspinall | 1899 | 4–4–2 | 19 × 26 (i) | 7 3 | 2,052·8 | — | 26 | 175 |
| 15. N.E.R. | W. Worsdell | 1900 | 4–6–0 | 20 × 26 (o) | 6 8 | 1,768 | — | 23 | 200 |
| 16. Midland | S. W. Johnson | 1901 | 4–4–0 | {(1) 19 × 26 / (2) 21 × 26} | 7 0 | 1,719·8 | — | 26 | 195 |
| 17. G.N.R. | H. A. Ivatt | 1902 | 4–4–2 | 18¾ × 24 (o) | 6 7½ | 2,500 | — | 30·9 | 180 |
| 18. G.W.R. | W. Dean | 1903 | 4–4–0 | 18 × 26 (i) | 6 8½ | 1,818·1 | — | 20·56 | 195 |
| 19. C.R. | J. F. McIntosh | 1906 | 4–6–0 | 20 × 26 (i) | 6 6 | 2,260 | — | 26 | 200 |
| 20. L.S.W.R. | D. Drummond | 1907 | 4–6–0 | (4) 16½ × 26 | 6 1 | 2,727 | — | 31·5 | 175 |
| 21. G.W.R. | G. J. Churchward | 1908 | 4–6–2 | (4) 15 × 26 | 6 8½ | 2,831·5 | 545 | 41·79 | 225 |
| 22. L.N.W.R. | C. J. Bowen-Cooke | 1910 | 4–4–0 | 20½ × 26 (i) | 6 9 | 1,547·1 | 302·5 | 22·4 | 175 |
| 23. N.E.R. | V. Raven | 1911 | 4–4–2 | (3) 16½ × 26 | 6 10 | 1,475·8 | 530 | 27 | 160 |
| 24. G.C.R. | J. G. Robinson | 1912 | 4–6–0 | 21½ × 26 (i) | 6 9 | 2,377 | 440 | 26 | 180 |
| 25. G.S. & W.R. | R. E. L. Maunsell | 1914 | 4–4–0 | 20 × 26 (i) | 6 7 | 1,520·6 | 335·1 | 24·8 | 160 |
| 26. G.W.R. | G. J. Churchward | 1914 | 4–6–0 | (4) 15 × 26 | 6 8½ | 1,841·3 | 283·1 | 27 | 225 |

NOTES:—(1) "The Duke" class. (2) "Precedent" or "Jumbo" class. (3) "Abbotsford" class. (5) "The Twelve Apostles." (6) Two-cylinder cross-compound; Worsdell–von Borries system. (7) "Teutonic" class; three-cylinder compound with one inside low-pressure cylinder. (8) Final design of "Gladstone" class; original engine appeared 1882. (9) Final design of Stirling eight-footer; original engine appeared 1870. (10) 3031 class. (12) First "Dunalastair" class; observe high proportion of boiler capacity to other dimensions. (13) No. 11, an isolated engine, 4-cylinder simple. (14) The "Highflyers." (16) Smith compound with one high-pressure and two low-pressure cylinders. (17) 251 class. (18) "City" class, finished by G. J. Churchward and fitted with his domeless taper boiler. (19) "Cardean." (20) No. 335, 4-cylinder simple; cross watertubes in firebox. (21) "The Great Bear," 4-cylinder simple first British Pacific type. (22) "George the Fifth" class. (23) 3-cylinder simple. (24) "Sir Sam Fay" class. (25) "Sir William Goulding"; isolated engine, at that time the largest passenger locomotive in Ireland. (26) Later "Star" class; original engine app[illegible]7.

Connemara train near Ballynahinch, Midland Great Western Railway, at the beginning of the century. The engine is Martin Atock's *Sylph*, a replacement of a similar but slightly smaller locomotive of the same name. The Galway-Clifden line was abandoned between the wars

## APPENDIX A—(*continued*)

## NOTEWORTHY BRITISH GOODS LOCOMOTIVES

### 1871–1914

| Railway | Designer | Date | Type | Cylinders | Driving wheels | | Evaporative heating surface | Superheater | Great area | Pressure |
|---|---|---|---|---|---|---|---|---|---|---|
| | | | | *inches* | *ft.* | *in.* | *sq. ft.* | *sq. ft.* | *sq. ft.* | *lb. per sq. in.* |
| 1. L.B.S.C. | W. Stroudley | 1871 | 0-6-0 | 17¼ × 26 (i) | 5 | 0 | 1,424 | — | 19·3 | 140 |
| 2. L.N.W.R. | F. W. Webb | 1873 | 0-6-0 | 17 × 24 (i) | 4 | 3½ | 1,074 | — | 17·1 | 140 |
| 3. G.E.R. | W. Adams | 1878 | 2-6-0 | 19 × 26 (o) | 4 | 10 | 1,393 | — | 17·8 | 140 |
| 4. L.N.W.R. | F. W. Webb | 1880 | 0-6-0 | 18 × 24 (i) | 5 | 1½ | 1,079·8 | — | 17·1 | 140 |
| 5. N.E.R. | T. W. Worsdell | 1886 | 0-6-0 | {(1) 18} × 24 (i) {(1) 26} | 5 | 1¼ | 1,136 | — | 17·2 | 160 |
| 6. Highland | D. Jones | 1894 | 4-6-0 | 20 × 26 (o) | 5 | 3 | 1,672 | — | 22·6 | 175 |
| 7. G.N.R. | H. A. Ivatt | 1900 | 0-8-0 | 19¾ × 26 (i) | 4 | 8 | 1,438·75 | — | 24·5 | 175 |
| 8. L.N.W.R. | F. W. Webb | 1901 | 0-8-0 | {(2)16 (2)20½} × 24 | 4 | 5½ | 1,753 | — | 20·5 | 200 |
| 9. Midland | H. Fowler | 1911 | 0-6-0 | 20 × 26 (i) | 5 | 3 | 1,170 | 313 | 21·1 | 160 |
| 10. G.C.R. | J. G. Robinson | 1911 | 2-8-0 | 21 × 26 (o) | 4 | 8 | 1,501 | 255 | 26·25 | 160 |
| 11. G.N.R. | H. N. Gresley | 1913 | 2-8-0 | 21 × 28 (o) | 4 | 8 | 2,084 | 570 | 27 | 170 |
| 12. S.D.J.R. | H. Fowler | 1914 | 2-8-0 | 21 × 28 (o) | 4 | 7½ | 1,321 | 360 | 28·4 | 190 |

NOTES:—(2) "Coal engine." (3) Design modified and completed by Massey Bromley. (4) "Cauliflowers." (5) Worsdell–von Borries 2-cylinder compound. (6) First British 4–6–0. (7) "Long Toms." (8) Four-cylinder compound. (10) Later engines had 180 lb. pressure; 521 examples built for Government in 1914–18 war.

## APPENDIX A—(continued)

## NOTEWORTHY BRITISH TANK LOCOMOTIVES

### 1872–1914

| Railway | Designer | Date | Type | Cylinders | Driving wheels | | Evaporative heating surface | Superheater | Grate area | Pressure |
|---|---|---|---|---|---|---|---|---|---|---|
| | | | | inches | ft. | in. | sq. ft. | sq. ft. | sq. ft. | lb. per sq. in. |
| 1. Festiniog | G. P. Spooner | 1872 | 0-4-4-0 | (4) 8½ × 14 (o) | 2 | 8 | 713 | — | 11·2 | 140 |
| 2. Midland | S. W. Johnson | 1875 | 0-4-4 | 17 × 24 (i) | 5 | 6 | 1,209·4 | — | 17·5 | 140 |
| 3. L. and Y. | W. Barton Wright | 1878 | 0-4-4 | 17½ × 26 (i) | 5 | 8 | 1,057 | — | 17 | 140 |
| 4. L.T.S.R. | Sharp Stewart | 1880 | 4-4-2 | 17 × 26 (o) | 6 | 1 | 1,020 | — | 17·25 | 160 |
| 5. L.B.S.C. | W. Stroudley | 1882 | 0-4-2 | 17 × 24 (i) | 5 | 6 | 1,029 | — | 15 | 140 |
| 6. Sligo L.N.C. | Beyer Peacock | 1882 | 0-6-4 | 16½ × 20 (i) | 4 | 9 | 972·3 | — | 14·9 | 130 |
| 7. Mersey | Beyer Peacock | 1887 | 2-6-2 | 19½ × 26 (o) | 4 | 7½ | 1,149·3 | — | 24·5 | 150 |
| 8. Taff Vale | T. Hurry Riches | 1888 | 4-4-2 | 17½ × 26 (i) | 5 | 3 | 1,272·7 | — | 19 | 160 |
| 9. Barry | Sharp Stewart | 1896 | 0-8-2 | 20 × 26 (o) | 4 | 3 | 1,476 | — | 22·75 | 150 |
| 10. G.E.R. | J. Holden | 1902 | 0-10-0 | (3) 18½ × 24 | 4 | 6 | 3,010 | — | 42 | 200 |
| 11. Cork B.S.C. | J. W. Johnstone | 1906 | 4-6-0 | 18 × 24 (i) | 5 | 2½ | 1,289 | — | 24 | 160 |
| 12. G.C.R. | J. G. Robinson | 1907 | 0-8-4 | (3) 18 × 26 | 6 | 8½ | 1,931 | — | 26 | 200 |
| 13. L.B.S.C. | D. E. Marsh | 1908 | 4-4-2 | 21 × 26 (i) | 6 | 7½ | 976 | 305 | — | 160 |
| 14. L. and Y. | G. Hughes | 1911 | 2-4-2 | 20½ × 26 (i) | 5 | 8 | 897 | 195 | — | 180 |
| 15. S.E. & C. | H. Wainwright | 1913 | 0-6-4 | 19½ × 26 (i) | 5 | 6 | 999 | 234 | — | 160 |
| 16. N.E.R. | V. Raven | 1913 | 4-4-4 | (3) 16½ × 26 | 5 | 9 | 1,058·8 | 273 | 23 | 160 |
| 17. L.B.S.C. | L. Billinton | 1914 | 4-6-4 | 22 × 26 (o) | 6 | 9 | 1,687 | 383 | 26·7 | 170 |

NOTES:—(1) "James Spooner," two motor bogies, 4 ft. 6 in. wheelbase at 14 ft. 2 in. centres, double-boiler Fairlie type. (2) Almost identical with Johnson's Great Eastern tanks of 1872. (4) Probably designed for Sharp Stewart by William Adams. (5) Stroudley's "D" tanks, identical except in boiler power with original design of 1873. (7) Condensing engines for underground work on heavy grades. (10) "Decapod" No. 20, an isolated engine. (12) For hump shunting at Wath-upon-Dearne. (16) Later converted to 4-6-2 type by L.N.E.R.

# LOCOMOTIVE AND ROLLING-STOCK LIVERIES OF THE BRITISH MAIN-LINE RAILWAY COMPANIES, 1914

In the following notes, the author has presumed in many cases to call the various standard colours by names which he considers most nearly descriptive, rather than by those quoted in official returns. The latter were often misleading, or indeed inaccurate; for example, London and South Western carriages were being described as "cream, with a yellowish tinge, above, and brown below,"30 years or more after this colour-scheme, or something like it, had been abandoned. The colours presently quoted are those in use at the end of the period 1874–1914, but notes are included on some of the earlier liveries, which readers are invited to supplement from their own records. In the following particulars, unless otherwise indicated, locomotive wheels were of the basic colour, buffer beams vermilion, and carriage roofs lead-white, weathering to grey.

## I. ENGLISH AND WELSH RAILWAYS

BARRY RAILWAY: Locomotives, dark red with polished brass dome casings and copper chimney caps, carriages, red.

CAMBRIAN RAILWAYS: Locomotives, black, lined yellow and red; carriages, bronze-green, lined yellow (until about the turn of the century, the green carriages had white upper panels).

CHESHIRE LINES: Carriages, oak-brown.

FURNESS RAILWAY: Locomotives, Indian red; carriages, dark blue with white upper panels and blue mouldings.

GREAT CENTRAL RAILWAY: Passenger locomotives, dark green, black and white lining, underframes (sometimes splashers and cylinder casings) dark red with vermilion lining; goods locomotives, black with red or red and white lines; carriages, varnished teak, some with polished brass lettering and figures. For locomotives a light yellow-green was in use in the 'nineties. In 1899, when the London extension was opened, carriages were brown with French grey upper panels, later changed to cream and finally discarded in 1910. Goods vehicles were lead grey. The Lancashire, Derbyshire and East Coast Railway had black locomotives, lined-out in yellow, red and blue; red carriages and lead-grey wagons.

GREAT EASTERN RAILWAY: Passenger locomotives, ultramarine blue, black borders, vermilion lines, polished brass beadings, coat of arms in cast iron on splasher, painted in full heraldic colours, lettering "G.E.R." in gold, blocked red, vermilion coupling rods; goods locomotives, black, vermilion lines, vermilion coupling rods; carriages, varnished teak; wagons, lead-grey. Various colour schemes were formerly used. Some Sinclair singles were painted yellow and known as "butter-flies." Johnson engines were green, including buffer-beams.

GREAT NORTHERN RAILWAY: Passenger locomotives, bright green, lined black and white with darker green edging on tender or tank sides, red-brown underframes lined vermilion, black cylinder jackets; goods locomotives after 1912, grey, lined white; Stirling engines and rebuilds, and the earliest Ivatt engines, had polished brass safety-valve casings; carriages, varnished teak; goods vehicles, red-brown.

GREAT WESTERN RAILWAY: Passenger locomotives, middle green, lined orange and black, black underframes, polished brass dome casings, safety-valve casings and beadings, copper chimney caps; goods locomotives the same green but without lining-out; passenger carriages, dark red; wagons, dark red, and grey. Before 1906, loco-motives had red-brown underframes, splashers and cylinder jackets, with tenders two- or three-panelled, the latter with "G.W.R." in copperplate script instead of the "Great Western" subsequently adopted. From the late 'sixties to 1908, carriages, originally chocolate all over, had cream upper panels; for four years, until 1912, all-over chocolate was reverted to. The red was discarded in favour of the old chocolate and cream after the 1914–18 war.

HULL AND BARNSLEY RAILWAY: Locomotives, "invisible green," very much the shade of dirty motor oil spilt on a road surface, i.e., black showing up green in certain lights; blue, vermilion and yellow lining-out, polished brass safety valves; carriages, varnished teak.

LANCASHIRE AND YORKSHIRE RAILWAY: Locomotives, black, lined in vermilion and white; passenger carriages, middle-brown above and dark purple-brown below, without panelling; wagons, dark grey.

LONDON AND NORTH WESTERN RAILWAY: Locomotives, black, lined red, with red and lunar-white (blocked yellow) lines on cab panel-plates, tender and tank sides, plain polished brass nameplates with black waxed letters, yellow-on-red cast-iron number-plates, black buffer castings and a black line forming a panel on the red leading buffer-beam; passenger carriages, purple-brown below waistline and on mouldings, white upper panels; goods vehicles, lead-grey. Up to the early 'seventies, locomotives were a bluish-green with black bands and highly ornamental chimney caps of polished steel, while the original Ramsbottom safety-valves were of brass, polished; Southern Division engines, under J. E. McConnell, were brick red, with copper-capped chimneys and brass dome casings.

LONDON AND SOUTH WESTERN RAILWAY: Passenger locomotives, light green, growing yellower in tinge as the present century advanced, with chocolate bands and black and white lines; passenger carriages, dark brown below waist with upper panels and mouldings in "salmon," a sort of brownish-pink that grew browner with age; ventilated milk and meat vans were "salmon" all over; wagons, dark brown. Up to about 1859, L.S.W.R. engines were Indian red with black bands; thenceforward to the early 'seventies, chocolate lined-out with black and white (also in vermilion on the best express engines); after about 1868 all new engines and many old ones had copper-capped chimneys and polished brass dome and safety-valve casings, previously present only on engines purchased from Beyer, Peacock and Co. Some double-framed engines had the outside frames painted vermilion. In the middle 'seventies the lining-out was changed on the express engines, and consisted of dark yellow edging divided from the chocolate by a thin white line. In 1878 William Adams substituted umber for the chocolate, with black bands and fine orange and pea-green lines; the red buffer-beams lost the black and white edging used by the Beatties. In 1885 Adams adopted pea green with black edging and white lines for new express engines, extending this to all his passenger engines and to rebuilt Beattie express engines in 1887. Goods locomotives and old engines, not rebuilt, were painted dark green with black edging and fine pea-green lines. This remained the goods livery until 1923. The London and South Western probably held the record for the variety of its locomotive liveries and for the number of times they were changed. Carriages were originally chocolate all over; many of Joseph Beattie's carriages were in varnished teak or mahogany; in the 'seventies new stock was painted brown with upper panels of a dark cream or green cheese complexion. Van ends were vermilion, then and for some years after.

LONDON, BRIGHTON AND SOUTH COAST RAILWAY: Passenger loco-motives, umber, lined yellow and black; goods locomotives, black, lined red; unaltered Stroudley locomotives had copper-capped chimneys; main-line passenger carriages, umber with white upper panels and umber mouldings and guard's van duckets; goods vehicles, grey. Under J. C. Craven, that is, up to the beginning of the 'seventies, locomotives were Brunswick green, lined black and white, with dark red underframes and platform angles, copper-capped chimneys and polished brass dome and safety-valve casings; very old engines with the wooden boiler lagging uncovered had this painted red and green for alternate planks; some had Wilson composite dome casings—red square base, green fluted-iron barrel, polished brass or copper top. Stroudley and R. J. Billinton painted passenger engines dark mustard-yellow ("Stroudley's Improved Engine Green") with olive-green edging, white, black and vermilion lines, claret-coloured underframes lined in white, black and vermilion, and buffer-beams with an ornate and elaborately lined vermilion panel imposed on claret-red; Stroudley goods engines were olive-green, and all his locomotives had his particular copper chimney cap, a work of art in itself. Prior to 1903, carriages were varnished mahogany with red ends; when the umber livery came in, the white panels were omitted from suburban stock, and, eventually, from all carriages. The umber locomotive livery was introduced, after some experiments with green, by D. E. Marsh, successor to R. J. Billinton.

LONDON, TILBURY AND SOUTHEND RAILWAY: Ordinary locomotives, bright middle green, lined black and white, red-brown underframes; there was an experimental application of a lavender-grey livery; condensing engines, available for working on to the District Railway, were black. Carriages, varnished teak. These liveries applied up to 1913, after which the Midland Railway painted the engines red, leaving most of the carriages unchanged. Electric cars, working on to the District, were at first dark green, later scarlet and brown.

MARYPORT AND CARLISLE RAILWAY: Locomotives green, some with brass safety-valve casings; carriages green with cream upper panels; wagons lead-grey.

METROPOLITAN RAILWAY: Steam and electric locomotives, dark red, lined-out yellow and black; compartment-type carriages varnished teak with cream upper panels; electric corridor stock, light oak brown with varnished teak upper panels. Locomotives were originally green, and later chocolate. In the 'sixties, and again at the turn of the century, dome casings were of polished brass.

METROPOLITAN DISTRICT RAILWAY (The "District"): Electric locomotives and cars, scarlet with chocolate strip at top and bottom, lead-grey roofs. In steam days, locomotives were olive-green with brass domes, and carriages reddish chocolate.

MIDLAND RAILWAY: Passenger locomotives, crimson-lake, lined black and yellow, red wheels under Johnson, black under Deeley and Fowler; goods locomotives, plain black; carriages, crimson-lake, lined yellow, lead-grey roofs with clerestory side-decks crimson. The crimson livery was of some antiquity for carriages, but until the middle 'eighties locomotives were bluish green, very like the pre-Webb engines on the London and North Western. Wagons were light lead-grey.

MIDLAND AND GREAT NORTHERN JOINT RAILWAY: "Golden ochre" (a light yellow-brown with an orange tint), lined light yellow and black; carriages, varnished teak. Of constituent companies, the Eastern and Midlands locomotives were originally green.

MIDLAND AND SOUTH WESTERN JUNCTION RAILWAY: Passenger locomotives, Midland red; goods locomotives, olive-green; carriages, Midland red.

NORTH EASTERN RAILWAY: Passenger locomotives, bright green, lined black, white and gold; goods locomotives, black, lined red; all had polished brass safety-valve casings and some express engines had narrow brass chimney caps. Green engines normally had black underframes lined in red, but one or two special engines, such as the famous departmental engine *Aerolite*, had red-brown underframes. In the 'eighties the locomotive livery had several variations; Gateshead engines were light green with bands of black and dark green, lined out in white and vermilion, while the underframes were red-brown, lined in vermilion; Darlington engines were lighter as to the green and had underframes of a darker brown; York engines were practically identical in colour with those of the Great Northern Railway, q.v.; Leeds engines were, prior to 1881, bright emerald-green, including the frames. Carriages, in later years, were a rich plum-red, with brown roofs; up to about 1879, first- and second-class carriages were a dark plum-red, and third-class carriages and vans were dark green; earlier still, coaching vehicles had white or cream upper panels, a legacy of the York, Newcastle and Berwick Railway. Wagons were lead-grey. The colour variations mentioned above were all inherited from constituent companies. In Edward Fletcher's day, enginemen were allowed, indeed encouraged, to embellish their engines as they pleased, within the bounds of propriety.

NORTH LONDON RAILWAY: Locomotives black, lined-out yellow and vermilion with blue-grey bands, red side-rods; carriages, varnished teak with vermilion ends to brake vans. During the Adams period, engines were bright green with polished brass dome-casings and safety-valves and polished copper chimney caps.

NORTH STAFFORDSHIRE RAILWAY: Locomotives, crimson-lake, lined yellow, black and vermilion; carriages, crimson-lake. At an earlier date, locomotives were "Victoria brown" and carriages had first cream and later white upper panels, which did not take kindly to the atmosphere of the Five Towns.

SOMERSET AND DORSET JOINT RAILWAY: Locomotives, dark blue with black and white lining; carriages, dark blue; wagons, dark grey. Before 1876, locomotives were dark green lined in yellow, and in the early days of joint ownership the Midland colours were used, locomotives being successively blue-green and red.

SOUTH EASTERN AND CHATHAM RAILWAY: Locomotives, 1912–14, dark green, lined yellow, red-brown underframes; previously, the green was lined-out in yellow, light green and vermilion and the underframes in yellow and vermilion; dome casings and manhole covers below safety-valves were of polished brass, and new express engines had chimney caps of polished brass or copper. Some goods locomotives were plain olive green. Carriages were reddish-maroon, and wagons dark grey. Of constituent railways, the South Eastern locomotives under J. I. Cudworth were painted the same as those of the Brighton under Craven; this green and red livery was probably a relic of the ancient locomotive pool once maintained by the London and Brighton, London and Croydon, and South Eastern companies; South Eastern carriages in early days were crimson. Under James Stirling, new locomotives were black or very dark brown, except the last (440) class which was green, and carriages were dark reddish-brown. London, Chatham and Dover locomotives were originally very similar in colour to those of the Brighton and the South Eastern, but the shade of the underframes was browner; William Kirtley, the last Chatham locomotive engineer, painted new engines black with yellow and vermilion lines and grey bands. Chatham carriages were varnished teak. Wagons were brick red on the South Eastern Railway and dark grey on the Chatham and the S.E. and C.R.

STRATFORD-ON-AVON AND MIDLAND JUNCTION: Locomotives, crimson-lake, lined in yellow, black frames; carriages, crimson-lake with cream upper panels lined-out in red and yellow.

TAFF VALE RAILWAY: Locomotives, black, lined-out in yellow, vermilion and white; carriages, chocolate with white upper panels. In early days, engines were blue-green; in the 'eighties, T. Hurry Riches painted his passenger engines red, with polished copper chimney caps and polished brass dome casings and safety-valve manhole covers.

WIRRAL RAILWAY: Locomotives, black, lined red and white; carriages, chocolate.

## II. SCOTTISH RAILWAYS

CALEDONIAN RAILWAY: Prussian-blue with red-brown underframes for both passenger and Westinghouse-fitted goods locomotives, lined-out black and white; ordinary goods engines were black with red lines, and sometimes with vermilion side rods; passenger engines had a lined-out vermilion panel on a red-brown ground for the buffer beam, with red-brown buffer castings. The blue varied in shade; originally it was a bright sky-blue, becoming darker in late Victorian times, but varying still; Perth produced a lighter blue than St. Rollox works. With the introduction of the large 4–6–0 locomotives of 1906, sky-blue was revived for some of the best express engines. Enginemen were allowed to decorate their locomotives with ornamental metal-work. Passenger carriages were brownish-lake, redder than the North Western brown, with white upper panels. Wagons were red-brown.

GLASGOW AND SOUTH WESTERN RAILWAY: Locomotives, middle-green with black and white lining, dark reddish-brown underframes; carriages, crimson-lake, like the Midland, and, in earlier years, green; wagons, lead-grey.

GREAT NORTH OF SCOTLAND RAILWAY: Locomotives, bright green with dark green edging, lined-out in black and vermilion; carriages, dark red with white upper panels (lacking in oldest vehicles); wagons, dark grey.

HIGHLAND RAILWAY: Locomotives, unlined olive-green all over, including buffer castings and buffer beams, becoming lighter in shade about 1912, when also the boilers of all but the latest express engines were painted black; David Jones's engines had narrow copper caps to their double chimneys. Carriages were olive-green, lined in yellow from 1903 to 1913; sleeping cars and saloon carriages were varnished teak ; passenger brake vans had vermilion ends, wagons brownish-red, In the late 'sixties, under William Stroudley, locomotives were in the same elaborate yellow livery as that used subsequently on the London Brighton and South Coast; at the beginning of the 'seventies, David Jones substituted light green for the yellow, retaining the dark red underframes and handsome lining out. In 1898, Peter Drummond introduced the well-known olive-green, but until 1903 edged it with dark green and black and white lines, keeping the dark red for the underframes and using a vermilion panelled buffer beam similar to that of Caledonian engines. During the Jones period, carriages were red-brown with green panels. From 1896 to 1903 the new green carriages had white upper panels.

NORTH BRITISH RAILWAY: Locomotives, dark brownish-green or very dark yellow, bordered in dark green, lined-out in yellow, black and vermilion, the same ground colour being used for the surround of the vermilion panel on the buffer beam and for the buffer castings; carriages were a rather flat purplish red, and wagons lead-grey. Until about 1876, locomotives were bright green, sometimes with polished brass dome and safety-valve casings, and carriages varnished teak; Dugald Drummond brought Stroudley's yellow from Brighton, but his lining-out lacked the thin vermilion line next the green border, having instead a double white line with black between; Drummond goods engines were olive-green. In the 'eighties, Matthew Holmes adopted the vermilion line and darkened the yellow; by the 'nineties, however, olive-green was being very generally used for passenger as well as goods engines. There followed another swing in favour of dark yellow, and the colour early in the present century was decidedly brown, of a pease-soup variety. These variations on, and mixtures of, the original Stroudley liveries developed, after our period, into a dark bronze-green, and goods engines were latterly black, lined yellow.

## III. IRISH RAILWAYS

BELFAST AND COUNTY DOWN RAILWAY: Locomotives, dark green, lined-out in white, black and vermilion; carriages, maroon with gold lines; wagons, lead-grey.

BELFAST AND NORTHERN COUNTIES RAILWAY: Locomotives, "invisible green" as on the Hull and Barnsley (q.v.), lined-out in yellow, blue and vermilion; some of the older engines had polished brass domes; carriages, dark-red lake, lined-out in vermilion and gold.

CORK, BANDON AND SOUTH COAST RAILWAY: Locomotives and carriages in various shades of olive-green, lined-out in yellow. Engines had brass domes and, in some cases, copper-capped chimneys; carriages were sometimes lighter in shade for the upper panels. The two American engines had Baldwin's standard iron dome-casing with a flanged base. Of constituent railways, the West Cork Railway had olive-green locomotives as on the then Cork and Bandon, but they were lined-out in black and vermilion.

COUNTY DONEGAL RAILWAYS: Locomotives black, lined vermilion; carriages brown, with white upper panels early in the present century.

DUBLIN AND SOUTH EASTERN RAILWAY: Locomotives, black, red bands and gold lines; carriages, crimson-lake, lined gold.

GREAT NORTHERN RAILWAY OF IRELAND: Passenger locomotives, green, lined-out in black and white or yellow, with vermilion background to brass letters and beadings of nameplates; goods locomotives, black with red lines; carriages, varnished mahogany or oak.

GREAT SOUTHERN AND WESTERN RAILWAY: Locomotives, black, lined-out red and white; carriages, purple-lake, lined out in yellow and red, sometimes (earlier in the century, and again, after our period, in the nineteen-thirties, with cream upper panels). Of constituent companies, the Waterford, Limerick and Western Railway had a livery almost identical with that of the Midland Railway in its later days, though some of the red locomotives had large polished brass dome casings, resembling those of the Great Western at that time.

MIDLAND GREAT WESTERN RAILWAY: Locomotives, emerald-green with black lines, vermilion ground to brass nameplates; carriages, brown with gold lines. Before 1903, the green engines were more or less elaborately lined-out in white and black; in that year an essay was made with a royal-blue livery for engines and carriages, with black and yellow lines for the former and white upper panels for the latter, but this was abandoned after about three years owing to the bad weather-resistance of the blue.

## SOME MINOR RAILWAY LIVERIES

The present author does not pretend that his record of railway liveries is complete, and its limitations become more apparent on consideration of the smaller railways. The following must be taken as a set of hand-picked specimens, and not in any way as an index. Apologies are offered in advance for omissions and for annoyance so caused.

CAMPBELTOWN AND MACRIHANISH LIGHT RAILWAY: Locomotives, olive-green, lined-out yellow, black and vermilion; carriages, olive-green with cream upper panels.

CENTRAL LONDON RAILWAY: Electric locomotives, chocolate; cars, chocolate with white upper panels; motor-cars had the louvres at the backs of the motor compartments picked out in vermilion.

CITY AND SOUTH LONDON RAILWAY: Electric locomotives at first chocolate, later panelled in dark yellow: cars chocolate.

CORK AND MACROOM DIRECT RAILWAY: Locomotives, black with red lines.

FESTINIOG RAILWAY: Locomotives and carriages, dark brick-red; some engines originally had polished brass domes (*Prince, Princess, James Spooner,* and the original *Taliesin*).

ISLE OF MAN RAILWAY: Locomotives, dark green, with black bands and vermilion lines; carriages followed variously, and simultaneously the styles of the London and North Western and the Lancashire and Yorkshire Railways (q.v.)

ISLE OF WIGHT RAILWAY: Locomotives, dark red, lined-out in yellow and black; carriages, varnished teak.

ISLE OF WIGHT CENTRAL RAILWAY: Locomotives, black, lined-out vermilion: carriages, varnished teak.

FRESHWATER, YARMOUTH AND NEWPORT RAILWAY: Locomotives, green with red coupling rods; carriages, varnished teak.

KENT AND EAST SUSSEX RAILWAY: Locomotives, dark blue, lined-out in white, black and vermilion; carriages, dark brown, panelled cream. *Tenterden, Northiam* and *Hesperus* had polished brass domes.

LYNTON AND BARNSTABLE RAILWAY: Locomotives, dark emerald-green, lined orange with black edging, polished brass dome casings and chimney caps, vermilion ground to nameplates, chocolate under-frames; carriages, dark brown with white upper panels.

MID-SUFFOLK LIGHT RAILWAY: Locomotives, dark red with copper-capped chimneys and polished brass dome casings.

NIDD VALLEY LIGHT RAILWAY (BRADFORD CORPORATION): 0–6–0 tank engine *Milner* was black with polished brass dome casing and copper chimney cap; carriages and wagons were variously dark red and brown, with the unfortunately ambiguous initials "B.C."

WATERFORD AND TRAMORE RAILWAY: Locomotives, green, with polished brass dome casings; carriages, red and (first-class) dark blue.

## *Appendix B*

## PULLMAN CAR LIVERIES

The old Pullman colour was a rich mahogany brown, very floridly decorated in gold-leaf. After the acquisition of the British Pullman Car Company by Sir Davidson Dalziel in 1906, cars were painted umber with cream upper panels (the umber strip at the top is of fairly recent introduction). On the South Eastern and Chatham Railway, Pullmans were dark red, and this colour was later applied to the two cars operated on the Metropolitan Railway extension line.

Index

*Hardwicke*, 151
Heating of carriages, 137–8
*Hecate*, 121
Helsingfors Station, 88
*Herod*, 54
Highland Railway, 23, 27, 68, 79–84, 106, 127, 141, 185
Holden, James, 38, 44, 114, 119, 129, 139
Holmes, Matthew, 23, 70, 71
Hook of Holland Express, 39
Hughes, George, 116
Hughes, John Ceiriog, 67
Hull and Barnsley Railway, 52, 180

Inchicore works, 88
Invalids, carriages for, 127
Invergarry and Fort Augustus Railway, 69
Inverness, 80
*Iron Duke*, 47
Iron Duke engines, 47, 103
Ironclad G.E.R. Engines, 106
Isle of Man Railway, 171–2, 188
Isle of Wight Central Railway, 165–6, 188
Isle of Wight Railway, 165–6, 188
Ivatt engines, 35
Ivatt, H. A., 88, 114, 116

*Jane*, 166
Jerome, J. K., 12
John Hick engines, 111
Johnson engine, 17, 114
Johnson, S. W., 31, 32, 107, 109, 113–14
Jones, David, 68, 81, 82, 106, 114, 115, 129, 131
Jubilee engines, L.S.W.R., 115
Jumbo engines, L.N.W.R., 22, 110

Karl-Ludwigsbahn (Galicia), 115
Kent and East Sussex Railway, 167, 188
Kessler, Emil, 115
Khartoum Station (Waterloo), 12
Kingsbridge (Dublin) Station, 88
Kings Cross Station, 34–5
Kirtley, Matthew, 18, 105
Kirtley, William, 43
Klondyke engines, 116
Knox, Mgr. R., 50
Kruger engines, 109

Lamb, Driver, 150
Lambie, J., 23, 117
Lancashire and Yorkshire Railway, 52–3, 126, 127, 180
Lancashire, Derbyshire and East Coast Railway, 52, 170
Lavatories in trains, 131
Leeds Northern Railway, 59
Leek and Manifold Valley Railway, 55
Leicester and Swannington Railway, 34
Light Railways Act, 166
Limerick Junction, 91
Listowel and Ballybunion Railway, 174–5
*Little Wonder*, 161
Liverpool and Manchester Railway, 29
Liverpool Overhead Railway, 54, 62
Liverpool Street Station, 11
Llanelly and Mynydd Mawr Railway, 66
Llantrisant, accident at, 63
Locke, W. J., 12
London and North Eastern Railway, 36, 60, 107
London and North Western Railway, 11, 19, 20, 22, 27–30, 32, 33, 38, 40, 46, 110, 127, 130, 132, 136, 138, 140, 141, 143, 146–7, 153, 180
London and South Western Railway, 11, 13–17, 26, 27, 29, 32, 33, 34, 44, 45–6, 104–5, 130, 135, 144–5, 146, 154–9, 181
London Bridge Station, 12
London, Brighton and South Coast Railway, 11, 17, 19, 23, 43–5, 125, 135, 139, 141, 181
London, Chatham and Dover Railway, 40, 41, 42–3, 144
Londonderry and Lough Swilly Railway, 173
London, Midland and Scottish Railway, 32, 38, 74, 107, 113
London, Tilbury and Southend Railway, 34, 39–40, 182
Long Charleys, 48, 126
Long Tom engines, 120
Loop Line, 55
Lundie, C., 64
Lynton and Barnstaple Railway, 163, 188

McConnell, J. E., 105
McDonnell, Alexander, 88, 90